"'What if dreams have value?' This question, which Dr. Kelly Bulkeley poses early in *The Spirituality of Dreaming*, piqued my curiosity. I've always had vivid dreams, many of which have felt revelatory or even prophetic, yet I've always dismissed my dreaming as having very little relevance to my day-to-day life. So Bulkeley's scientifically researched thesis, bolstered by stories of religious, spiritual, and historical practices from cultures around the world, has felt mind-shifting. Dreaming as a tool for social transformation: Who knew? This eye-opening book feels deeply hopeful, and I may never sleep the same way again."

—**Karen Walrond,** author of *The Lightmaker's Manifesto* and *Radiant Rebellion*

"While reading *The Spirituality of Dreaming*, I kept deeming it a sheer privilege to be led into the strangely familiar offline world we enter each night by so learned and lucid a guide as Kelly Bulkeley. As the leading researcher on dreams and dreaming in world religions, he amiably captures here a lifetime of scholarship in this pulsating, personal, playful invitation to delve into rich spiritual possibilities generated by our dreams. This is a brave and beautiful book. Prepare to be moved and enlightened."

—**Robert C. Dykstra,** author and Charlotte W. Newcombe Professor of Pastoral Theology, Princeton Theological Seminary

"Filled with both research evidence and personal examples, *The Spirituality of Dreaming* is one of the most intriguing and fascinating books I've read. Kelly Bulkeley leads us inside of the world of dreams and illustrates how our dreams offer spiritual healing to us and others. Dreams serve as a portal to and from the divine and provide another opening for the Spirit to lead us home."

—**Lerita Coleman Brown,** spiritual director
and author of *What Makes You Come Alive:
A Spiritual Walk with Howard Thurman*

"Calling all dreamers! In this compelling, beautifully written book, dream researcher Dr. Kelly Bulkeley makes a persuasive argument that dreaming can be cultivated as an intentional spiritual practice. In addition, dreaming is essential for leadership; if we want lives that are Spirit-led and Spirit-filled, we must listen closely to the language of our dreams. This book weaves together cutting-edge evidence, ancient wisdom from faith traditions, and practical techniques that readers can utilize in everyday life. This book has offered me deeper understanding and a renewed commitment to take my dreams seriously!"

—**Kate H. Rademacher,** author
of *Reclaiming Rest: The Promise of
Sabbath, Solitude, and Stillness
in a Restless World*

"*The Spirituality of Dreaming* makes clear why Kelly Bulkeley is one of the foremost dream researchers—if not *the* foremost— in the field of the psychology of religion and spirituality. He reminds us of the power of spiritual dreaming, that dreaming is fundamentally a spiritual practice for 'a culture that has fallen dangerously out of touch with its own dreaming resources.' The book will appeal to scholars and researchers, as well as to the general reader interested in envisioning better possibilities for the future, even 'when apocalyptic threats are looming on all sides.'"

—**Kirk A. Bingaman,** author and
professor of pastoral mental health
counseling, Fordham University

"*The Spirituality of Dreaming* offers clear guidance to connecting with the creative and deeply personal power of the dreaming mind, through the well-presented methods of science, culture, and tradition. Kelly Bulkeley reminds us that sleep is an absolute essential, and he invites us to become more active players in the meaningful drama of our dreaming lives. I thoroughly enjoyed the journey."

—**Michelle Carr,** assistant research
professor, University of Montreal

THE SPIRITUALITY
OF DREAMING

THE SPIRITUALITY
OF DREAMING

*Unlocking the Wisdom
of Our Sleeping Selves*

KELLY BULKELEY

Broadleaf Books
Minneapolis

THE SPIRITUALITY OF DREAMING
Unlocking the Wisdom of Our Sleeping Selves

Library of Congress Cataloging-in-Publication Data

Names: Bulkeley, Kelly, author.
Title: The spirituality of dreaming : unlocking the wisdom of our sleeping selves / Kelly Bulkeley.
Description: Minneapolis, MN : Broadleaf Books, an imprint of 1517 Media, [2023] | Includes bibliographical references.
Identifiers: LCCN 2023009976 (print) | LCCN 2023009977 (ebook) | ISBN 9781506483146 (hardcover) | ISBN 9781506483153 (ebook)
Subjects: LCSH: Dreams. | Spirituality. | Self-actualization (Psychology) | Dream interpretation.
Classification: LCC BF1078 .B785 2023 (print) | LCC BF1078 (ebook) | DDC 154.6/3—dc23/eng/20230505
LC record available at https://lccn.loc.gov/2023009976
LC ebook record available at https://lccn.loc.gov/2023009977

Cover image: © Adobe Images; Panoramic Fantasy Cloudscape by SoulMyst
Cover design: Cindy Laun

Print ISBN: 978-1-5064-8314-6
eBook ISBN: 978-1-5064-8315-3

CONTENTS

CONTENTS

PART III
ASPIRATIONS

INTRODUCTION

At no point during childhood did I ever say, "When I grow up, I want to be a *dream researcher!*" Even if I had known such a thing was possible, it would have held zero interest to me. Raised in a middle-class California suburb in the 1960s and 1970s, I was an outward-focused kid, directing all my energies toward school, friends, riding my bike, building forts, and participating in the yearly calendar of sports—football in the fall, basketball in the winter, baseball in the spring and summer. Anything involving competition and a ball: that's where you would find me. I didn't think much about the future beyond fantasies of playing center field for the San Francisco Giants. I just assumed things would work out, that I would find a way to support myself and continue living as I always had. In retrospect, I can recognize the many privileges built into that easy assumption. At the time, it just felt like the natural and obvious way to go. All I had to do was keep trying to win in the classroom and on the playing field, and everything else would take care of itself.

A hint that I might eventually decide to depart from the path of normality came in fifth grade, when I was about eleven years old. Our teacher had assigned us a special writing project of two or three pages on any topic we liked, and a friend and I cowrote a twenty-page paper on the history of horror movies. We analyzed the classic films of Western horror by decade (1920s–1960s), profiled the top actors, and ranked the movies in various categories. We received not only the highest grade in the class but one of the highest grades the teacher had ever given for any assignment. Score! Something clicked, and it was something beyond mere competition. I can now see how my passion for research and writing was kindled by this project. I can also understand what I found so compelling about the subject of scary movies. The top three films in my eleven-year-old pantheon of cinematic horror were *Frankenstein* (1931), *Dracula* (1931), and *King Kong* (1933)—all of which appeared just before the imposition of the Hays Code in 1934, which strictly prohibited "vulgarity and suggestiveness" in American movies for the next thirty years. I had no idea about that at the time, of course, but I definitely sensed in my top three an opening into a realm of forbidden insights and uncanny truths. Other people seemed to find movies like that weird and scary, but I was intuitively drawn to them and wanted to explore them in more depth.

At some point during adolescence, I began noticing that I was having vivid and recurring nightmares. Or more accurately, I could no longer *ignore* that for many years, I had been having vivid nightmares. They usually involved being chased by a variety of terrifying antagonists—wild animals, monsters, aliens, murderous humans—and never being able to escape, no matter what I tried to do. As I thought more carefully about these recurrent dreams and their persistent themes of fear, aggression, and vulnerability, I marveled at their dramatic complexity and overwhelming energy. They clearly related to the movies I had watched throughout childhood, but the dreams were scarier and even more intense than the films, and they were bizarrely interwoven with a wild variety of images, emotions, and characters. How, I wondered, could these terrifying, hyperrealistic experiences emerge from my own sleeping mind?

I began reading books about dreams—everything I could find, old and new, famous and obscure, scientific and mystical. I also began keeping a dream journal, tracking the metamorphoses of my nightmares over time. The practice of writing my dreams in a journal on a regular basis added structure and focus to my efforts to understand the private horror movies playing nightly in the theater of my imagination.

After a while, I noticed something was happening, something quite unexpected. My dreams seemed to be *changing* in response to my waking interest and attention. The recurrent scenario of being chased had diminished in frequency and intensity, and other themes came to the fore. What did this gradual but unmistakable change mean? After more reading, reflecting, and dreaming, I realized a kind of dialogue had emerged between the conscious and unconscious aspects of my mind. It was as if two parts of myself were carrying on a dialogue mediated by dreams.

This surprising discovery sparked an enduring curiosity about dreams and a desire to learn more about them. I wanted to understand not just what I could learn from this dialogue with my dreaming self but what it meant that such a thing was possible at all. What kinds of beings are we that in waking, our minds function in one way, and in sleep they function so very differently? And if we found a way to integrate these two aspects of ourselves more fully, what kinds of beings could we *become*?

We Need Your Dreams

Fast-forward about forty years and here I am, a dream researcher, someone professionally devoted to the study of dreams. I have written many books and academic articles about dreams, and I manage an open-access digital archive, the Sleep and Dream

Database (SDDb), with a collection of more than fifty thousand dream reports from a wide variety of sources.

I could never have gotten here without the many teachers, friends, and colleagues who helped and encouraged me along this extremely unconventional path. In this book, I will share with you the best insights and practices I have learned from these wise guides about how to enhance your innate capacities as a dreamer. Whether or not dreams have been an important part of your life before now, *The Spirituality of Dreaming* will give you the keys to unlock new dimensions of your own nocturnal imagination.

To be clear from the outset, this book will also speak honestly about the challenges and difficulties that come with dreaming. It is important to be aware of both aspects, the positive and the negative, if you want to develop your dreaming powers to their fullest extent. The biblical story of Joseph and his brothers provides a dramatic expression of the potential perils in the life of a dreamer: "They saw him from a distance, and before he came near to them they conspired to kill him. They said to one another, 'Here comes this dreamer. Come now, let us kill him and throw him into one of the pits; then we shall say a wild animal has devoured him, and we shall see what will become of his dreams'" (Gen 37:18–20). All three of the great Abrahamic religions—Judaism, Christianity, and Islam—include Joseph's story in their sacred texts. In each of these traditions, he is held up as an ideal model of a dream interpreter: someone whose pure faith in God enabled him to understand symbolic dreams. His greatest success was interpreting the Pharaoh's dreams about the coming famine, which none of the other sages, diviners, and magicians of Egypt could figure out. However, Joseph's career as a dream interpreter would never have begun but for his narrow escape from his murderous brothers. His power as both a dreamer and the interpreter of the dreams of others emerged within a context of acute danger and mortal threat.

If you have also experienced vivid, highly symbolic dreams, you can sympathize with Joseph's ordeals. Perhaps you, too, were treated differently early in your life because of your weird dreams and active imagination. People might have said there was something wrong with you, something not quite normal, maybe a problem with how your brain works. Perhaps you noticed it when someone became disturbed or even frightened by what you said about your dreams. At some point, you realized that most other people just don't dream like you do.

The Spirituality of Dreaming is written for you. You might be unusual, but you are not alone. There have been people like you—big dreamers—in every culture around the world and in every period of history. There are big dreamers in the contemporary world, too, and in this book, you will learn about their best insights and teachings. Whatever natural dreaming talents you already possess, there are ways for you to enhance and develop them further. My hope is to inspire you to honor and respect yourself as a dreamer and to recognize the latent powers within you.

I also hope this book will lead to new self-discoveries for you even if you do not consider yourself a big dreamer. These same powers of spiritual dreaming are latent within you too. Maybe you are a person who used to have vivid, memorable dreams but no longer does. Maybe you're someone who remembers your dreams fairly often, but they seem to have no special meaning, like they're just rehashing mundane thoughts from current life. Still, you're curious. You sense more is possible in your dreams, more than your waking mind currently understands. But the access is blocked by a paradox: How can you get beyond the limits of your own consciousness to reach those deeper insights? *The Spirituality of Dreaming* is written for you too. The beauty of dreaming as a spiritual practice is that it provides a universally accessible experience in which your waking ego naturally recedes, allowing the creative powers of your unconscious psyche to come forth. The power of spiritual dreaming is available to everyone, every night when we sleep, throughout our lives. Wherever and whenever you start the journey, your dreams are there, ready to respond to the gift of your conscious attention.

Let me be honest: I am offering these insights and teachings not just for your personal improvement, although that's a good thing too. My real goal is to recruit you for a bigger cause. The fact is *we need you*. Your community needs you, right now. If you are a big dreamer, your visionary gifts can make a real contribution to the collective health of those around you in these fraught and perilous times. It's a good thing that big dreamers can be found in every culture and period of history because they are essential to collective survival, especially in periods of extreme fear and uncertainty. Intensified dreaming gives people the ability to look beyond the seemingly insurmountable limits of present reality. It enables them to envision new approaches to current problems, articulate the enduring values of the community, and stimulate others to draw more deeply upon their own creative resources.

As we confront apocalyptic threats looming on multiple fronts, the practices and insights developed by big dreamers around the world are directly relevant to our troubled circumstances today. *The Spirituality of Dreaming* is a call to action for all the dreamers of the modern world. It asks you to take yourself seriously as a dreaming visionary and to recognize the value of your emergent powers.

It asks you, in short, to embrace a life of *spirit*.

Cultivating the Spirit

In every known religious and spiritual tradition around the world, dreams have been regarded as a valuable means of communication between humans and the divine. As we shall see in the coming chapters, dreaming has played an important role in a variety of religious beliefs and practices, especially around the themes of healing, prophecy, creativity, and death. Some philosophers have speculated that dreaming is itself the origin of religion—that the core ideas of a disembodied soul, an afterlife, supernatural beings, and otherworldly realms all first emerged in human consciousness via dreaming. This is certainly the case with individuals who have converted to a religious tradition like Christianity, Islam, or Buddhism because of a powerful dream experience. In modern, mostly secular Western society, it might seem strange to connect dreaming with religion. But in the broad sweep of human history, dreaming and religion have always interacted with each other. What's strange is our contemporary amnesia about this time-honored relationship. I'm one of many who want to change that—and like I said, we need your help.

In this book, I am using *spirituality* as a synonym for *religion* in the sense of beliefs about the ultimate nature of human life and our relations with transpersonal powers. The term spirit will be used in a very specific way, as a principle of vital movement, of movement that both expresses and generates life. We hear of this in the *Ruach Elohim* of Genesis 1:2, the "spirit" or "wind" or "breath" of God that moved over the face of the waters in the dark and formless chaos just before the creation of the world. We hear of it in the *psyche* of ancient Greek mythology and philosophy, the dynamic totality of our individual being whose essence, according to Aristotle, is motion. We hear of it in the Latin word *inspirare*, "to breathe" or "to blow into," a reference to the rhythmic flow of air in and out of the lungs. We hear of it in the *geist* of German philosophers like G. W. F. Hegel and Friedrich Nietzsche, the concept of life as constant dialectical unfolding and self-realization. Spirit, in this sense, can take religious and nonreligious forms. It can manifest in quiet personal contemplation and in large group activities. It reflects a vivid awareness of the primal forces that animate our existence, drive our growth, and fuel a process of continual self-transcendence.

Interestingly enough, spirit in this sense is also connected to the biological concept of *irritability*, which is the capacity of living organisms to respond to stimuli in their environment. If you poke something that is alive, it will usually react with some sort of movement. If you poke an inanimate object, there is no such autonomous response, no self-directed movement. Spirit is the difference between life and death. It is the ability to act, to change, to become something new, to self-transcend. Dreams, and especially nightmares, can be powerful sources of "irritating" stimuli, poking us in parts of our personalities we have neglected or avoided and prompting us to move toward greater awareness, integration, and growth. Toward a life of greater spirit.

This quality of open-ended dynamism is what originally drew me to the study of dreams. As I began reading about dream teachings and insights from other cultures and earlier periods of history, I realized these questions extend far beyond the conceptual framework of modern Western psychology. If I wanted to learn about the dimensions of dreams that most interested me, I would have to broaden the perspective and include the findings of many different fields of study. Hence my decision to pursue graduate study in divinity schools, in programs that combined religion and psychology. I am not a conventionally religious person, but I knew that for most of human history, people had thought of their dreams in religious terms. So I hoped that gaining a deeper knowledge about the history of religions would help me better understand these traditional ideas about dreams and how they relate to modern scientific research. You will see my approach in action in the coming pages as I move back and forth between religious and psychological approaches, always centering on the lived experience of the dream.

The thesis of this book is simple: Dreaming can be cultivated as a spiritual practice. While your body lies motionless in bed, your spirit soars. To be a big dreamer is to live a life of spirit. It might seem that an intense inward focus on dreaming and spirit is a recipe for social withdrawal, but that's not true. A life of dreaming and spirit can unfold in a variety of social settings, with deep involvement in communal activities and interpersonal relations. And to live a life of spirit will inevitably place you in positions of *leadership*: positions where you can have a meaningful impact on the well-being of other people. To be a spiritual leader, as the phrase will be used in this book, means leading *from* spirit and leading *toward* spirit. It means drawing on your powers of spirit to guide your actions in the world, and it means helping other people develop their own powers of spirit. True spiritual leaders, at least as I have known them in my life, are characterized by humility, concern for others, and openness toward transpersonal powers and otherworldly realities. Spirit begets more spirit.

Here is an important lesson to draw from the story of Joseph's life as a dreamer. It was for just this reason that his brothers doubted his sincerity and plotted to murder him.

A few lines earlier in the story, we hear what prompted their ire against their younger sibling: "Now Joseph had a dream, and when he told it to his brothers they only hated him the more. He said to them, 'Hear this dream which I have dreamed: behold, we were binding sheaves in the field, and lo, my sheaf arose and stood upright; and behold, your sheaves gathered round it, and bowed down to my sheaf.' . . . Then he dreamed another dream, and told it to his brothers, and said, 'Behold, I have dreamed another dream: and behold, the sun, the moon, and eleven stars were bowing down to me'" (Gen 37:5–9). His brothers had an immediate, angry interpretation of these dreams: Their younger sibling was suggesting that they bow down to him, that he was to have dominion over them. They saw his dreams as a direct threat to the traditional family order. The only motivation they could imagine for his behavior was a selfish desire for power. They did not recognize the possibility of an ego-transcending divine calling. Instead of discerning the mysterious movements of spirit, they could only see a challenge to their position, and they tried to destroy it. Their response, while harsh, is not entirely surprising. It is not the first, nor even the second, fratricidal plot in the book of Genesis. Earlier chapters relate the stories of Cain murdering Abel and Esau trying to murder Jacob. In both cases, an older brother is enraged at a violation of primogeniture, and he fights violently to restore the privilege of the eldest son to receive the blessings of the father. Joseph's brothers are essentially doing the same thing for the same reason.

But Joseph did not die, as they plotted. In and through his dreams, he rose above them, not to rule them but to serve as their beacon in an increasingly dangerous and uncertain future.

The Ultimate Dream Guide

The chapters in part I of this book look at specific methods that big dreamers have developed to enhance the insightfulness of their dreams. These include approaches to healthy sleep, techniques of interpretation, keeping a dream journal, and sharing dreams with others. In part II, we will look at three realms of dreaming where spiritual energies can be especially strong: in dreams of animals and nature, gods and demons, and death and dying. The third and final part of the book explores the furthest reaches of spiritual dreaming, drawing on both ancient religious teachings and modern science to consider dreams as a means of expanding consciousness, a source of inspiration for art and cultural change, and a potential ally in the development of new technologies for health, healing, and connection.

I can promise that reading this book will help you develop a more dynamic relationship with your dreaming self, a relationship that will continue to grow and benefit you for the rest of your life. It's not that I have any special magic to bestow; it's that you have tremendous spiritual powers within your dreams, powers that can transform your waking life and contribute to collective change. I will offer ideas and practices that can help you gain more conscious access to these powers. Ultimately, however, you don't need me or anyone else to tell you where to go. The farther you move along this path, the more clearly your own dreams will illuminate the way ahead.

Part I

Practices

CHAPTER 1

A Revolutionary Act
Sleeping

The story of creation in the book of Genesis ends with the curious image of God resting (*shabbat*): "And he rested on the seventh day from all the work that he had done" (Gen 2:2). It seems like an obvious instance of anthropomorphism in the Bible's portrait of God's character, in which authors attribute finite human qualities (such as being tired) to an infinite divine being. God possesses the awesome power to create heaven and earth and yet still needs to take a break from work? How does that make sense? It can't be a matter of simply replenishing God's energy. An omnipotent deity presumably has inexhaustible power, and several biblical passages assert that God never wearies or gets tired.

Some commentators believe the "rest," or *shabbat*, of God in this passage from Genesis is not about a biological need for recovery but a formal statement about the process of creation, specifically its end. At the end of the six days of creation, God *stopped* creating. The "rest" of God means nothing other than this conclusion of divine world-building activity, this climactic moment of completing the cosmogonic process. Ceasing the work of creation is a moment so singularly important that God blessed and hallowed it.

Yet I still find it interesting to consider the possibility that God *did* need to rest following the creation. Perhaps God needed rest in the sense of a temporary withdrawal from external activity: a focus on quiet, internal rejuvenation that leads to a renewed capacity to engage with the outside world. In other words, perhaps God *slept*. What would it mean to conceive of hallowed, blessed *sleep* as an integral part of divine creation?

Sleep provides the vital foundation for spiritual dreaming, so we shall begin here. The world of sleep is full of curious paradoxes. It is both deeply grounded in our physical nature and thoroughly shaped by our family and cultural communities. It is both a normal, ordinary part of life and a strangely complex and multifaceted realm of experience. It is both an intimately personal form of inward withdrawal and a powerful means of actively working on the problems and challenges of the waking world. Indeed, in our relentlessly active 24/7 world, affirming the values of sleep has become a revolutionary practice.

This is the essential claim of Arianna Huffington's 2016 book *The Sleep Revolution: Transforming Your Life, One Night at a Time*. Huffington has become a self-described "sleep evangelist" on behalf of both the health benefits of sleep and its spiritually renewing power. After a lifetime of relentlessly fast-paced work and travel with the least possible sleep she could get away with, Huffington realized she was driving herself into the ground. Her physical health, mental sharpness, and emotional balance were all suffering, and she realized she had to make a change— quickly. So she pledged to herself that for a whole month, she would sleep at least eight hours a night. The results were transformative, enabling her to feel something she had not felt for many, many years: a sense of being truly well rested. Huffington says, "When we are asleep, the things that define our identity when we're awake—our jobs, our relationships, our hopes, our fears—recede. And that makes possible one of the least discussed benefits (or miracles, really) of sleep: the way it allows us, once we return from our night's journey, to see the world anew, with fresh eyes and a reinvigorated spirit, to step out of time and come back to our lives restored." Her emphasis on this "miracle" of sleep is helpful in highlighting the spiritual potentials in this fast-changing area of scientific research.

The Sleep Cycle

That we need sleep is a biological fact; *why* we need sleep remains an open question. To sleep is not the same as lying motionless with your eyes closed in a dark room. Sleeping is not simply the absence of physical and mental activity. It brings on a dramatic shift in the functioning of the brain and body, a shift with important connections to internal activities involved in memory and learning, digestive health, and the immune system. In some ways, sleep can be characterized as a period of recovery from yesterday's labors; in others, it can be conceived as a period of preparation for tomorrow's challenges. This underscores the fundamentally cyclical nature of sleeping and waking. We cannot understand either without understanding both in their dynamic interrelatedness.

The new field of chronobiology has found a surprising variety of ways in which our bodies depend on the natural rhythm of sleeping and waking, with the timing of various processes determined by the setting and rising of the sun. Having evolved on a planet that spins around a star, we humans, along with all other terrestrial life forms, depend on a regular flow from one state to the other, from existence in the light of day to existence in the shadows of night. Our bodies have been designed by evolution to function best within that circadian flow (the word *circadian* combines the Latin *circa*, "around," with *diem*, "day").

Chronobiology has shown, for example, that vital hormones from the immune system are released during specific phases of sleep. If sleep is disrupted during those times, it can effectively block the hormonal releases, harming the health of the whole body. Researchers in this field have also found that disruptions to the timing of when we eat in relation to when we sleep can make an enormous difference in healthy digestion and weight maintenance. Irregular sleep, insomnia, overeating, and obesity have a mutually reinforcing and negative relationship. Clinicians are paying more attention to these chronobiological cycles, too, because, for example, the timing of when a medication is administered can make a huge difference in how the patient's body metabolizes it. The same medicine can be half as effective if taken at one time of day versus another.

New discoveries in chronobiology have accelerated greatly since 2017 when the Nobel Prize in Physiology or Medicine was awarded to Jeffrey C. Hall, Michael Rosbash, and Michael W. Young for, according to the Nobel press release, "their discoveries of molecular mechanisms controlling the circadian rhythm." These investigators found that specific genes, possessed not only by humans but also by other animals and plants, have the capacity to keep track of the time of day, enabling them to trigger various bodily processes at their optimal moment of functioning. According to Satchin Panda in his 2018 book *The Circadian Code*, a "big breakthrough" for scientists in the field came with this basic finding: "We are born with a strong circadian clock that instructs every aspect of our body to work efficiently. It sets a daily rhythm for when to sleep and wake up, eat, and be active. We are at our best health when we are living at a pace that aligned with this perfect rhythm."

At least three insights from chronobiology have special significance. First, sleep is a natural, healthy, and non-optional part of life. Perhaps there are organisms somewhere that do not depend on sleep, but we humans certainly do, and we should be skeptical of anyone who devalues sleep or dismisses its importance. Second, sleep is rhythmic. It involves regular, repeated cycles of activation throughout our minds and bodies, and it links us to bigger rhythms of day and night, light and darkness, outer and inner realities. Our optimum health and vitality emerge from this steady drumbeat of sleeping, waking, sleeping, waking, sleeping, waking. Third, sleep is active, not passive. It only *seems* passive from the standpoint of the waking ego. The brain does not simply shut down when we slumber; it shifts its energies and activities to other modes of functioning. We apparently need the ego to retire and go offline for sleep's nocturnal work to proceed. In this way, learning more about sleep can introduce you to the unconscious, non-ego dimensions of your own psyche.

Customs of Sleeping

Sleep may be natural, but it is never *only* natural, at least for us humans. Our sleep behaviors inevitably arise within a social context and are shaped by cultural, political, and economic conditions that permeate our lives. Even when we close our eyes at night to sleep, we remain thoroughly social and socialized beings. An excellent book, *Sleep Around the World*, edited by Katie Glaskin and Richard Chenhall in 2013, presents various ways humans across cultures have organized their sleeping behaviors. One factor that jumps out from these examples is that most cultures consider co-sleeping with other people as the norm. As Roger Lohmann notes in his participant-observations with the Asabano people of Papua New Guinea, sleeping with other members of the village is a matter of group protection and social companionship; inviting others to sleep in your home is considered "basic hospitality of the same order as providing shelter." Among the Asabano, the co-sleeping instinct becomes more intense during times of collective crisis: "Whenever there was some kind of stress, I observed early on, people gathered in the community house to sleep together in solidarity against the witches and nature spirits who cause illness and death."

Compared to the Asabano and the other cultures surveyed in *Sleep Around the World*, we in the modern West have developed the unusual practice of sleeping alone in isolated rooms. There are variations and exceptions, of course, with co-sleeping among romantic partners, siblings, parents and children, and students in dormitories. But few other cultures prioritize as we do the private bedroom. To be clear, this is not necessarily a good or bad thing. Cultural variations are just that: variations. Humans have found many different ways to satisfy their basic need for sleep, and the point here is to highlight the distinctive cultural values built into each of these customs. In the modern West, we tend to emphasize the values of individual autonomy and personal privacy, and we have built those values into our architectures of sleep.

In addition to influencing where and with whom we sleep, culture also impacts *when* we sleep. Most of our slumber occurs at night, of course, but daytime sleep such as napping also plays an important role in many people's overall sleep life. In some cultural traditions—in Latin America and parts of the Mediterranean, for example—public and commercial activities temporarily stop each afternoon as people follow their midday meal with a light nap or *siesta*. This custom reflects a wise adaptation to the warm climate of these regions, helping to protect people from the worst heat of the daytime sun. It also reflects an awareness that humans typically experience a lull or slight dip in energy in the early afternoon, and they will benefit if allowed a brief amount of time for rest. Not surprisingly, the cultural values embedded in these traditional practices have often clashed horribly with the values of industrial capitalism, starting in the late eighteenth century in Europe. A demand for strict accounting of time and labor meant workers were increasingly forced to align their sleeping-waking cycles with the clock time of factory production. In this new industrialized view, no value is given to midday sleep and no latitude granted for natural variations in circadian flows of energy. In the long history of violent conflict between workers and capitalists around the world, this painful disruption of traditional patterns of waking and sleeping has surely played a role.

What Kind of Sleeper Are You?

The nature-culture dynamic of sleep is also characteristic of other primal activities such as eating, drinking, grooming, communicating, and procreating. Something we have evolved to do becomes, through culture, an expression of distinctive human values. In today's hyperstimulating world, it can be easy to forget that sleep is indeed one of our vital needs—until a painful accident or illness forces the issue. Much better than ignoring your sleep needs is paying attention to your own personal dynamic of natural sleep needs and cultural sleep traditions and finding as much of a steady rhythm between the two as you can manage.

Here is an opportunity for increased self-awareness. Take a moment to consider the following questions.

* Are you a lark or an owl? Are you an early-to-bed, early-to-rise person, or do you wake up slowly and feel more energetic at night? Neither is better than the other, but it helps to know what you are so you can avoid or minimize, if possible, involvement with social systems that clash with your chronobiological type.

* Are you a long or short sleeper? Most adults do well with seven to nine hours of sleep per night, depending on the time of year. Some people are fine with six hours per night, but anyone who regularly sleeps less than that is increasing their risk of long-term health problems. Other people prefer ten hours per night or more, which can be fine for some, although excessive sleep can sometimes be a symptom of depression.

* Are you a light or heavy sleeper? Are you easily woken out of sleep, or do you sleep so deeply that you find it difficult to wake up? Sleep tends to be heaviest in childhood and become lighter and more fragmentary as we get older. But age is not destiny, and sound sleep can often be preserved throughout life if a consistent, lifelong rhythm can be maintained.

* Are you a monophasic or polyphasic sleeper? If you generally sleep all the way through the night, with no daytime naps, then you are a monophasic sleeper. If you

have long periods of waking during the night or if you regularly take naps during the day, you are a polyphasic sleeper. Again, neither is better than the other; they are simply natural variations on the basic need for a healthy amount of sleep.

Your answers to these questions form your own personal baseline of sleep. Knowing more about your fundamental characteristics as a sleeper will help you find the best conditions possible for your personal sleep needs. Just as importantly, more awareness of your own sleep needs will enhance your awareness of *other* people's sleep needs. Once you become sensitized to the factors that impact your sleep, you will begin to see how those factors impact the sleep of people all around you. The path to a healthier culture of sleep for everyone begins with this insight.

Anomalies

Sleep may be natural and healthy, but it can also be extremely weird. Strange and unsettling mind-body experiences can occur in sleep—what researchers call *parasomnias* and what children call "things that go bump in the night." Some of these have clear roots in the physiology of sleep, while others are more perplexing in their origins.

Two of the most common parasomnias are sleepwalking and sleeptalking. These phenomena can occur together or apart, and they tend to appear in the first half of the night, when the brain is primarily in slow wave, or non-rapid eye movement (REM) sleep. Sleepers have no conscious awareness of what they are doing or saying during these episodes, and they rarely have any memory of their behaviors in the morning. Sleepwalkers can occasionally get themselves into trouble by wandering into dangerous situations, but usually they just shuffle around near their beds before settling down again. The big danger with sleep-talking seems to be the possibility of unconsciously revealing an embarrassing secret to someone nearby, although that kind of self-disclosure rarely happens. In general, the verbiage that comes from the sleeptalker meanders from one topic to another, with little direct or sustained responsiveness to any inputs.

Less common but more dramatic when they do occur, night terrors and sleep paralysis can elicit alarming responses in both sleepers and those around them. The two form something of a mirror to each other: night terrors usually appear in the first half of the night, with intense physical reactions but no consciousness, while sleep paralysis tends to occur in the second half of the night, with the body still asleep but the mind partly awake, which often generates intense feelings of confusion and fear. As is true with many parasomnias, night terrors and sleep paralysis are most common in childhood and adolescence and taper off or disappear entirely in adulthood, although an experience of sudden stress can prompt sleep disturbances at any time of life. Parents who have seen their children in the throes of a night terror know how frightening and uncanny it looks from the outside. The child's eyes may be wide open and they might be sitting up in bed, screaming at the top of their lungs, and yet they are clearly nonconscious and unresponsive to any attempts at comfort. Then, after a few moments, they lie down again and fall asleep and remember nothing of it in the morning. The parents, however, cannot forget having seen their children in such obvious distress. Parents often have a hard time shaking the idea that something must be terribly wrong to cause such a bizarre thing to happen in the middle of a child's sleep.

The same is true with episodes of sleep paralysis. In addition to the body's immobility, sleep paralysis often includes a vivid sensation of someone else being in the room with the sleeper, someone who should not be there. This menacing visitor tends to be a shadowy figure who assaults the sleeper physically and sometimes sexually. Different cultures have given specific names to these malevolent beings. The traditional people of Newfoundland speak of a supernatural being, the Old Hag, who attacks people in their sleep. People in agrarian cultures of medieval Europe told stories of the incubus: a demonic being who preys on people while they sleep, sitting on their chests and squeezing the breath from their lungs. In ancient Jewish traditions, men are warned against the she-demon Lilith, who attacks during their sleep when they have no power to resist her. For more on the spiritual dimensions of these experiences, Ryan Hurd's 2010 book *Sleep Paralysis: A Guide to Hypnagogic Visions and Visitors of the Night* is an excellent guide. As Hurd notes, some researchers point to contemporary claims of alien abduction as having the same basic characteristics as sleep paralysis: the individual is usually alone in bed, conscious but immobile, when they are suddenly assaulted by an unknown being. This particular parasomnia offers an especially good example of how a natural phenomenon of sleep can become woven into a culture's distinctive system of meanings and values.

Beyond illustrating the intertwining of nature and culture in sleep, this quick tour through the curious world of parasomnias will hopefully plant two ideas in your mind that will grow and expand in the coming chapters. The first is fairly simple: What we think of as "normal" sleep is anything but. It turns out that humans have a tremendous range of variation in sleep patterns among individuals and groups, along with great variation within individuals over the course of their lives. Although frightening parasomnias like night terrors and sleep paralysis afflict large numbers of people, the episodes usually do not have a pathological cause, nor do they generally have any damaging effect on the sleeper. They are not unhealthy or harmful; they are just, to put it simply, *weird*. As such, they illustrate how our definition of healthy sleep needs to be much broader and more flexible than we might have assumed, allowing for multiplicities of experience rather than asserting a single standard of normality. The second idea that emerges in this overview of parasomnias is how easily they lend themselves to religious and philosophical reflections. When people experience these strange variations of sleep, they almost inevitably wonder about their deeper causes, meanings, and implications. Parasomnias, in other words, are a natural source of spiritual reflection.

So before getting into anything specifically having to do with dreams, we start by recognizing the power of sleep—even weird sleep—to stimulate questions about existential topics: the nature of consciousness, the relationship between the mind and the body, the dynamics of time and space, the existence of non-human supernatural beings, and the ability to travel in alternative realities. Humans have traditionally understood that sleep is potentially a realm of spiritual discovery in which the power of waking ego essentially disappears and new dimensions of the self and the world open up.

In many cultures around the world, people see the nightly experience of an ego-free state of being as an invitation to the spiritual dimensions of life. In these settings, sleep itself is regarded as a sacred practice. Sleep experiences that are frightening and upsetting are especially likely to provoke urgent spiritual reflections. When we experience such mysterious, haunting phenomena, we tend to seek a bigger framework in which to make sense of them.

Why Do We Devalue Sleep?

Alas, present-day Western society does not consider sleep a sacred practice. Far from it. Those of us who live within this broad cultural ecosystem are encouraged to view sleep in negative terms, focusing primarily on what it does *not* involve. When we are sleeping, we do not work, shop, consume, travel, party, communicate, or use social media. Sleep is a desert of action, an annoying interruption of our most important, productive, and enjoyable activities.

Is there a deeper cause for this modern devaluation of sleep? We could attribute it to the Protestant work ethic that sociologist Max Weber believed was the true motivation for the "spirit of capitalism." The intense anxiety of Protestants about the predestined fate of their eternal souls led them, according to Weber, to work intensely not for worldly gain but to demonstrate, through overwhelming economic productivity and financial success, their status among God's chosen ones. Thus, the unrelenting and dehumanizing churn of work in capitalist societies has its roots in a particular system of theological beliefs about how God relates to humans.

Not all capitalists are Protestant, however, nor all Protestants capitalist, so other, nonreligious factors must be at work in the cultural depreciation of sleep. In strictly business terms, the human need to sleep has been perceived as an obstacle to economic efficiency. That attitude has prompted labor unions in many different industries to fight for the allowance of reasonable amounts of time for sleep in workers' lives, especially for employees in sensitive and dangerous professions like truck drivers, airline pilots, and healthcare staff. Businesses almost always battle against these kinds of changes in labor rules until the cost of accidents caused by sleep-deprived employees becomes too harmful to the bottom line. Sleep researcher William Dement of Stanford University devoted much of his career to educating politicians and the general public about the horrible accidents, injuries, and disasters that have occurred as a direct result of workers not getting enough sleep. Thanks to his efforts, attention to sleep has become a regular part of workplace safety considerations for employees in many parts of the economy.

And yet the cultural pressures against sleep continue—and even accelerate. In addition to religious and economic forces, we can also point to new digital technologies, especially in the areas of entertainment and social media, as powerful contributors to an ethos of constant wakefulness. With a vast and ever-expanding selection of movies and television to watch, video games to play, and online discussions to follow, many of us now detach ourselves from the regular alterations of day and night and live in a perpetually wakeful (and chronically sleep deprived) *now*. These new technologies are designed to encourage ever greater use—which means discouraging ever turning them off. This becomes a big problem at night, when the time comes to sleep. The television show episode ends on a cliffhanger, so you want to watch the next episode; you're super close to leveling up in your favorite video game; something outrageous pops up on your social media feed, and you're curious to see the funny things people say in response. Before you know it, you have stayed awake for several hours longer than you intended, and it is now even harder to fall asleep after all that bright stimulation.

The cultural devaluation of sleep in the modern world has many sources, not just one. It appears that religious, economic, and technological forces each play a powerful role in diminishing people's attention to the value of sleep. If this is the case—if we live in a society that pushes and nudges and prods people in countless ways to stay awake and avoid sleep—it raises important questions: Who benefits from these conditions? Whose interests are served by having a society filled with sleep-deprived people?

Sleep as Resistance

Among the predictable effects of chronic sleep deprivation are weakened mental functioning, diminished physical coordination, muted interest in other people, and neglect of one's surroundings. People who are sleep deprived tend to become increasingly obedient, compliant, and noncommunicative. They can still perform repetitive tasks and routine procedures, but they lose the capacity to innovate and adapt to new circumstances. In effect, they become less human and more robotic. This is the reason sleep deprivation so often serves armies and police forces as a form of nonviolent torture: it quickly disrupts the most fundamental rhythms of our minds and bodies, breaking down resistance and, if pushed to extremes, producing excruciating pain and long-lasting physiological damage. In less extreme forms, a group of moderately sleep-deprived people will still be functional in basic ways but with drastically reduced capacities for independent thought and creativity and a greater willingness to accept the comforting routines of the status quo.

So the simple answer to the question of who benefits from our sleep deprivation is: anyone who wants to hold power over someone else. It does not require an especially conspiratorial mind to see the potential for social exploitation in this. The more sleep deprived people become, the less capable they are of resisting, protesting, or even questioning the authorities who govern their lives. They lose their mental sharpness and become more vulnerable to political misinformation, financial scams, authoritarian ideologies, and workplace abuses. Their interpersonal skills diminish, making it harder to maintain normal social relationships and empathize with others. All in all, a population of chronically sleep-deprived people is a dictator's dream: a flock of docile, atomized, minimally demanding sheep.

In this context, asserting the value of sleep takes on the qualities of a revolutionary act. To advocate for the importance of healthy slumber is to defy the cultural forces of modern society that depreciate our basic need for sleep. This might seem like a minor or trivial form of resistance. But it actually represents a direct challenge to one of the key strategies used by any oppressor—namely, disrupting people's biorhythms—and it offers a practical means for renewing people's agency and autonomy in the world. If you can take back control of your sleep, you can take back control of your mind and body, and this will in turn enhance your health and vitality in ways that serve *your* interests, not someone else's. As you restore the natural circadian flow of your life, you become a much more formidable human being: stronger, quicker, more creative, more self-determined. You are less likely to be a pushover for bullies and frauds and more likely to innovate new solutions to collective problems.

Evidence can be seen of growing movements of defiance toward the anti-sleep ethos of many modern social systems. Although most of the examples I offer in this book come from English-speaking North America and Europe, as they are the areas of my greatest familiarity, the basic issues here extend to other parts of the world too. An especially vivid instance of radical sleep advocacy comes from contemporary China, with the *tang ping*, or "lying flat," movement. A young ex-factory worker wrote a manifesto in April 2021 titled "Lying Flat Is Justice," in which he rejected the cultural norms of endless work, status competition, and empty consumerism. Instead of a life driven by frantic activity, people can choose to simply lie flat on the ground and enjoy the world as it is, sleeping as much as their minds and bodies need. The idea of *tang ping* has found a surprisingly large and receptive audience in a society where many people hold jobs in the "996" system, in which they are expected to work from 9:00 a.m. to 9:00 p.m. for six days a week. As a cultural ideal, a 996 work schedule is plainly inconsistent with most people's basic chronobiological needs. From a social policy perspective, giving up some sleep may seem worth the sacrifice if it leads to greater overall economic productivity, but that can be a tricky bargain. Pushing people to work so long and hard can indeed increase their output in some ways, but we know from modern sleep research that it will not make them more innovative—quite the opposite, in fact. Those who get inadequate sleep tend to be markedly less creative, flexible, and adaptive when responding to new circumstances. They are *not* the people you want leading a corporate innovation team. A full accounting would have to balance whatever gains a 996 work schedule (in China or anywhere else) produces with the likely increase in accidents and injuries, the time lost to worker illness and medical problems, the rise in alcoholism and substance abuse, the undermining of family relationships and stability, and the long-term physical and mental health damage. As advocates for an alternative cultural ideal, members of the *tang ping* movement seek to reorient their life goals and aspirations according to their simplest, most vital physical and emotional needs, the foremost of which is sleep.

Another focus of revolutionary sleep activism here in the United States is the "nap ministry" of Tricia Hersey, an artist and theologian in Atlanta who has developed a variety of programs and workshops around the concept that "rest is resistance," which is also the title of her 2022 book. She highlights the historically rooted forces of racism, misogyny, and capitalist exploitation as they have combined to constrict people's sleep, especially Black people in America, especially Black women. Hersey goes beyond a purely sociological critique to frame the problem as a religious crisis. She speaks of sleep as a portal to a renewed awareness of our inner spiritual potential:

> Sleep deprivation is a public health issue and a spiritual issue. . . . We have been trained to believe that everything we accomplish is because of our own pushing alone. This is a false because there is a spiritual dimension that exists in all things and in everything we do. To understand that we are spiritual beings navigating life in a material world opens us to the possibilities of rest as a spiritual practice. Our entire living is a spiritual practice. Much of our resistance to rest, sleep, and slowing down is an ego problem. You believe you can and must do it all because of our obsession with individualism and our disconnection to spirituality. Nothing we accomplish in life is totally free of the influence of spirit and community. We do nothing alone.

We should also note that businesses have long recognized the potential to wring huge profits from sleep. Sales in the United States of pillows and mattresses now constitute a multibillion-dollar industry, dominated by a handful of large corporations. These companies have a built-in incentive to amplify, through their marketing, the perils of sleep deprivation and the value of a good night's slumber—which they can guarantee for you if you're willing to buy a new mattress for the approximate cost of a decent used car. Critics claim the peddlers of various sleep-enhancing products have been exaggerating the problems of sleep deprivation just to boost their sales. The charge of advertising excess may be true, yet the underlying problems of inadequate sleep in the modern world are real, especially for those at the lower end of the social and economic hierarchy. Studies suggest that insomnia, or the inability to sleep, is more frequent among women than men, younger people than older people, Black and Hispanic people than Whites, and people with lower annual income than those with higher annual income. There seems to be a directly proportional relationship between sleep quality and social location—a relationship, to be clear, that is not natural but largely cultural. These differentials in the quality of sleep among different populations reflect our collective values and choices. As a social good, sleep is unfairly distributed in American society in ways that are grimly familiar.

Hersey demonstrates admirable spiritual leadership in calling for greater attention to the living history of sleep deprivation in America:

> We believe rest is a form of resistance and name sleep deprivation as a racial and social justice issue. . . . This is about more than naps. It is not about fluffy pillows, expensive sheets, silk sleep masks or any other external, frivolous, consumerist gimmick. It is about a deep unraveling from white supremacy and capitalism. These

two systems are violent and evil. History tells us this and our present living shows this. Rest pushes back and disrupts a system that views human bodies as a tool for production and labor. It is a counter narrative. We know that we are not machines. We are divine.

Divine Slumber

When I first began a serious study of dreams, I focused on their qualities as a type of religious experience, comparable to meditation, ritual, mysticism, trance, and other forms of altered consciousness. I soon realized that what distinguishes dreaming from those other mystical phenomena is its grounding in the natural rhythms of sleep. Dreaming is the most *democratic* of religious experiences in the sense of its universal accessibility. No special training, secret knowledge, or ascetic behaviors are required to dream; no preconditions limit access to an elite few. Because everyone sleeps, everyone is a dreamer—or at least has the potential to become one.

In this way, scientific research on sleep is directly continuous with and supportive of a spiritual approach to dreams. To learn about the farthest reaches of the dreaming imagination, we begin by paying close attention to the basic patterns of our nightly sleep. That has been a guiding insight for my whole career, and it has motivated this chapter's effort to frame the rest of the book within this dynamic relationship between sleep and dreams.

Instead of a one-way process—using sleep research to promote dreaming—perhaps now we can also use dream research to promote better sleep. Among the many predictable consequences of inadequate sleep is diminished dream recall. Of course, if you assume that dreaming has no value, you won't consider a loss of dreaming a negative consequence. But if dreaming *does* have value, then we should be alarmed by anything that disturbs, diminishes, or eliminates it.

And what of the question with which we started this chapter: Does God sleep? Stories about the gods of the Greek pantheon portray them as periodically sleeping, and so do myths about the deities of India, China, and Egypt. Most monotheistic religions, however—Jewish, Christian, and Muslim sources—emphasize that God is essentially tireless, boundlessly energetic, and perpetually vigilant and thus has no need for sleep.

I wonder if this belief in divine wakefulness might change somewhat if it were brought into dialogue with our present-day understanding of sleep. Sleep is not *non*activity but a different *kind* of activity; it is woven into and interconnected with a host of other activities. We see dynamic cycles of vital energy coursing throughout creation, at every level of reality we can perceive. Why should we assume that God's activities are limited to what humans do during the day? Why assume that God does not *want* to sleep? And if God sleeps, why wouldn't God dream too?

Some Christians today are using the phrase "God's dream for the world" as an alternative to the traditional image of "God's kingdom on earth." Bishop Desmond Tutu made this vision— *God's Dream of the World*—the title of his book for children, which shares Tutu's profound faith in the future that God dreams for all of us. This might sound like a merely metaphorical use of *dream*, but as you will see in the coming pages, actual dreams have these same qualities of integrating differences, anticipating a better future, and inspiring practical actions in the present. If God is truly dreaming of us and for us, it means God cares about us, deeply. It means we exist within God's sphere of concern and that our unfolding lives are actualizations of what God has dreamed we will become. And it means we are all blessed with a divinely sanctioned inner guide for this lifelong process—namely, our own core human capacity for spiritual dreaming.

CHAPTER 2

Fraught with Truth
Interpreting Our Dreams

We are all dreamers, every one of us: high and low, rich and poor, young and old. One of the first Christians to advocate for this key spiritual insight was Synesius, a leader of the early Christian church in what is present-day Libya. He taught that dreams have great value as a primary source of religious experience. Dreaming is a spiritual phenomenon, he maintained, and one that transcends all social boundaries and divisions. Synesius agreed with other ancient philosophers who also recognized dreaming as a portal of communication between people and the gods. But he went beyond most of his contemporaries in highlighting the all-embracing inclusiveness of spiritual dreaming. The idea that all people could have inspired dreams was a theme he found harmonious with the new Christian message of welcoming all people to the faith, even those from the most marginal parts of society. Synesius saw dreaming as the natural ally of a religion whose central animating creed is God's love for all of humankind.

Unfortunately, when the institutional church began to organize, define, and codify its official theological beliefs, the universalist dream teachings of Synesius were not included. On the contrary, church authorities went out of their way to designate dreaming as a type of forbidden sorcery, akin to witchcraft or astrology. Many centuries later, however, Synesius's insights have finally received validation. Modern researchers have shown that dreaming is indeed rooted in brain-mind processes shared by all human beings. Every time we sleep at night, our brains go through a complex cycle of activation, including several phases of high neurological arousal, known as REM sleep. This term comes from the fact that while the brain is extremely active, the body is paralyzed—all except the eyes, which dart around under the lids. Some researchers refer to this phase as paradoxical sleep because it is a very deep sleep in some ways and a very light sleep in others.

No matter what term we use, this phase of sleep is closely related to the experience of dreaming. If you awaken someone from the midst of REM sleep, the person is more likely (80 percent of the time, according to several estimates) to remember a dream than if you awaken them from non-REM sleep. Now to be clear, people remember dreams from non-REM sleep too—about 40 percent of the time—just not as often as they do in REM sleep. This means that while REM sleep does not *cause* dreaming, it does provide a reliable *trigger* for it. And everyone has several phases of REM sleep every night, whether or not we remember those experiences when we awaken. We are all dreamers, then, at least potentially. We are all born with a brain-mind system that generates a regular stream of dreaming experience as part of its normal, natural, healthy functioning. Synesius was right: the creative power of dreaming is innately accessible to everyone, everywhere.

But dreams can be difficult to understand. The oracle may indeed come to us all, as Synesius claimed, but she speaks in a very cryptic language. Few people in contemporary society have been taught anything about the nature or meaning of dreams, so whenever they *do* recall a dream, it poses a genuine challenge. You may feel this whenever you remember a new dream. Where should you begin in trying to interpret this strange expression of your nocturnal imagination? What should you focus on? How do you know if you are on the right track? When, if ever, will you discover the true meaning of the dream—and how will you know? Is there just one "correct" interpretation of a dream? There are no easy answers to these questions, and even asking them in certain settings can make others raise their eyebrows. No wonder so many people conclude that dreams are nothing but random nonsense.

And yet I believe that not only are we all natural *dreamers*; we are natural dream *interpreters* too. The basic skills involved in exploring, analyzing, and understanding the meanings of our dreams are within reach of everyone, from all backgrounds. We have an innate capacity both to dream and to make sense of dreams. Every time I teach a class or workshop, most people in the group make the surprising discovery that they are actually pretty good at interpreting dreams. Having such a skill is something they never knew about themselves. Present-day society gives us few opportunities to exercise and develop this ability, but it is a powerful potential within us all.

The process of interpreting dreams starts with the *recall* of dreams and the realization that not all dreams are the same. They vary in length, form, content, theme, and intensity, which leads to the principle that different types of dreams often require different approaches to their interpretation. Some dreams seem so transparent, so obvious in their meanings, that no interpretation is required. Other dreams overflow with complex images, cryptic symbols, and strange emotions. In most cases, new insights come from looking at one's dreams as expressions of the deeply rooted human capacity to think *metaphorically*: to make sense of the world in terms of creative metaphors. As we learn how to understand the metaphors of our dreaming imaginations, we enter a potentially transformative spiritual dialogue.

To Sleep, Perchance to Dream

If you are sleeping in a laboratory and a lab technician awakens you during a REM phase, you will probably remember a dream. If you are not artificially awakened but continue to sleep through the night, however, you may not recall that dream the next morning. Is an unremembered dream still a dream? That's a tough philosophical question. Another tough question is this: if we normally forget so much of our dreaming each night, are the bits we do remember merely arbitrary fragments—flotsam from the mind's nocturnal activities that happen to wash up on the shore of waking consciousness in the morning?

Here as much as anywhere in life, people form judgments based on their personal experiences. Someone who has little or no dream recall can find it hard to appreciate that many other people are high recallers who frequently have lively, colorful, richly detailed dreams. Fortunately, we can now refer to publicly available survey data with thousands of people's answers to questions about their dream recall. That data can help us move beyond personal assumptions to a more evidence-based understanding of who remembers their dreams and how often they do so.

The big-picture view looks like this: About half the population of American adults remembers a dream at least once a week or more often. The other half of the population recalls their dreams less often than once a week. A small percentage (around 8 percent) of people say they remember their dreams almost every time they wake up, while a slightly smaller percentage (around 6 percent) say they rarely or never recall their dreams. In terms of demographic factors, age seems to have the biggest impact on dream recall. Younger people tend to remember dreams much more often than older people do. We do not have enough historical or cross-cultural data to tell if this decline in dream recall over the lifespan applies to people in all places and times, or if it stems from some specific cultural factor in modern society, or if it involves some combination of the two.

In terms of gender, women tend to remember more dreams than men do, but the difference is small, and some studies have found equal levels of dream recall in men and women. No studies to date have looked at the dream recall frequencies of nonbinary people, but a student in a class I recently taught did some research on this topic for their final paper, and they found that dream recall rates for nonbinary people are basically the same as the rates for men and women. No studies have looked at dream recall among people from different sexual orientations, either.

Race and ethnicity do have an impact, however, with Black people having slightly higher dream recall than Whites, and Hispanic people having higher recall than both. Other demographic factors like education, income, and regional location do not seem to have any influence on dream recall. This underscores an important point: dream recall is a steady feature of human experience no matter who we are, where we come from, or what our identity may be. Here is more evidence to support Synesius in his claim about the sacred universality of dreaming.

That being said, some studies have pointed to a few specific factors that seem correlated with higher dream recall. For instance, psychoanalyst Ernest Hartmann's research found that people with what he called "thin boundaries" had higher dream recall than do people with "thick boundaries." Hartmann's concept of psychological boundaries tries to account for a basic difference in how people relate to the world. Some of us insist on making clear, sharp distinctions between reason and emotion, individual and group, and right and wrong, while other people need a more fluid sense of moving between and among these kinds of polarities. The former, Hartmann says, are people with thick psychological boundaries, and they are less likely to take an interest in dreams. People with thin boundaries, however, tend to have fewer limits on images and energies from their unconscious entering their conscious awareness. This, naturally, correlates with higher dream recall (and also with artistic creativity and vulnerability to mental illness).

Consistent with this distinction between thin and thick boundaries, other researchers have found that higher dream recall is associated with the personality trait of "openness to experience." In studies I have conducted over the years, I have found that higher dream recall also correlates with an individual's concerns about global warming, support for the Black Lives Matter movement, and liberal or progressive political views generally. In other words, people with progressive views tend to have higher dream recall than others.

Now, to be clear, these correlations are *not* absolute. Some people who hold conservative views and have thick psychological boundaries also frequently remember their dreams. And some people with very liberal views and thin boundaries have little or no dream recall. But it does seem significant, particularly when we are discussing a spiritual approach to dreaming, that dream recall seems to be highest among people who are vividly aware of their connections with other people, other forms of life, and the world as a whole.

Big Dreams

People remember a wide variety of different types of dreaming, what psychologist Harry Hunt calls the "multiplicity of dreams." The simplest distinction we can make between different types of dreams focuses on the intense memorability of a few dreams. Some dreams simply feel much more meaningful and important than others. Many cultures and religious traditions through history have made a basic distinction between significant and insignificant dreams, according to the degree of their experiential impact on the dreamer.

Psychoanalyst Carl Jung had this distinction in mind when he spoke of "little" and "big" dreams. Little dreams relate to the normal activities of our daily lives; they are not meaningless, but they tend to revolve around mundane concerns and ordinary situations. Big dreams, however, leave ordinary reality far behind. They include hyper-vivid images, feelings, characters, and interactions that often differ drastically from anything in the dreamer's waking life. They occur most often in childhood but can arise at any time of life, especially during periods of stress or transition. Jung famously said this about these remarkable expressions of the nocturnal imagination: "Big dreams are often remembered for a lifetime, and not infrequently prove to be the richest jewel in the treasure-house of psychic experience."

In a study I did in 2013 with Ernest Hartmann—he of the thin-thick boundary distinction—we compared "most memorable" dreams with "most recent" dreams: that is, the dreams people report when asked, "What's the most recent dream you can remember?" We found that the highly memorable dreams had more "primal" content than the most recent dreams: more family and animal references, more aggression and fear, and more of both misfortunes and good fortunes. These results led me to seek a more precise way of mapping the kinds of dreams that people report most frequently in response to the question "What is the most memorable dream you have ever experienced?" Using the findings from the research with Hartmann as a foundation, I began to explore the possibility that big dreams tend to take a few specific forms. In effect, I was looking at the rarest dreams to find their most common types. Based on research from neuroscience, content analysis, anthropology, and the history of religions, I found four frequently reported kinds of highly memorable dreams—what we can call *prototypes* of big dreaming.

1. *Aggressive.* Many people's most memorable dreams are harrowing nightmares involving physical aggression, fear, violence, and death. The intensity of these dreams can be measured by their *carryover effects*: how the physical feelings from the dream (racing heart, fast breathing, sweating, clenched muscles) remain vividly in awareness for a few moments after awakening. Each of the four prototypes has a characteristic carryover effect.

2. *Sexual.* The physical intensity and realism of certain sexual dreams, combined with their unusual or taboo qualities, make them enormously impactful on people's waking awareness. Although it can be difficult to pursue

44

research on dreams with sexual content (more on that later), we know this is a regular feature of dreaming across cultures, among all human populations. Sexually charged big dreams often revolve around the perennial tensions between individual sexual desires and social restrictions on sexual behavior.

3. *Gravitational.* Gravitational dreams include dreams of falling, of things collapsing, of endless misfortunes, of the end of the world. This theme of decline and disaster generates its own kind of nightmare, with fear and terror mingling with confusion and sadness. At its most extreme, this prototype transforms into what I call *titanic* dreams: an otherworldly drama of cosmic entropy, with alien settings and vertiginous clashes of elemental force, mass, momentum, and space.

4. *Mystical.* All around the world and throughout history, people have reported intensely memorable dreams of magical flying, seeing dead people alive again, transcendent beauty and harmony, and other kinds of normally impossible, incredibly positive phenomena. In contrast to the downward pull of gravitational dreams, the inspiring prototype of mystical dreams envisions the many ways in which we can defy entropy, rise above the limits of ordinary reality, and let our spirits soar in radically new directions.

Highly memorable dreams can contain combinations of two or more of these prototypes, or they can fit in none of these categories and have different themes entirely. This four-part mapping does not, of course, represent a complete survey of all types of big dreams. For now, that goal remains on the distant horizon as researchers have only just begun to develop new theories based on the full range and potentiality of the dreaming imagination. Yet we can say with confidence that many people's big dreams have the characteristics of one or more of these four prototypes.

Increasing Your Dream Recall

By now, you may be recalling your own highly memorable dreams and thinking about how they relate to what I have said so far. I hope so, as you will certainly find this book more interesting and enjoyable if you keep a few of your own big dreams in mind as you read.

People often ask if it is possible to increase their dream recall. Here, for a change, the answer is simple and straightforward: Yes! Research has shown that people tend to remember more dreams when they adopt a more favorable view of dreams. For example, if you hear something positive about dreaming from a friend, a news article, or a book, your dream recall is likely to increase. Dream recall is basically a function of one's attitude, and attitudes can change. If you believe dreams are random nonsense, you are less likely to remember them than if you believe dreams are meaningful expressions of emotional or spiritual truth. The positive stimulus in waking life can be very slight for a noticeable effect to occur in dream recall; just shifting your attention a little more toward your dream life is often all it takes. Listening to a podcast about dreams, for example, or reading a dream-related blog post, or watching a movie with vivid dream scenes—simple things like these can have a big stimulating effect on dream recall. Perhaps the challenge is not how to remember more dreams but how to diminish non-dream distractions.

Sigmund Freud had a simple answer for why people have so much difficulty remembering their dreams. According to Freud, dreams express repressed unconscious desires in disguised symbolic form, precisely for the purpose of deflecting attention from your conscious mind. If the desires were allowed expression without the symbolic disguise, you would be so disturbed that you would wake up, and the healthful function of sleep would be ruined. This is why dreams are not meant to be remembered, in Freud's view; they are meant to vent repressed unconscious energies while preserving the peaceful conditions of sleep. In this view, a successful dream is a forgotten dream.

As has happened with many of Freud's ideas, modern researchers have found better answers for some of the dream-related topics he addressed (for instance, variations in dream recall seem to depend on factors like advancing age, the shift in brain states from sleeping to waking, and the conditions of awakening). But much of what Freud observed in human dreaming experience remains remarkably accurate and insightful. Anyone who says Freud's work is entirely outdated probably does not know much about either Freud or current dream research. On this particular issue of dream recall, we do not have to accept his whole psychoanalytic theory of dreams as wish fulfillment to appreciate this critical point he makes: that people tend to resist unpleasant truths about themselves, which leads them to create psychological defenses to protect against facing those truths. If Freud is right about that, then another significant factor in low levels of dream recall is humans' strong unconscious bias toward forgetting especially upsetting—and psychologically revealing—types of dreams. In its most extreme form, this leads to a bias against *all* dreams as a defense against anything that might emerge from the unconscious.

For our interest in dreaming and spirituality, Freud's insights about resistance offer a valuable reminder that making an active effort to explore your dreams will inevitably lead to surprising, startling, and occasionally shocking discoveries about yourself. Instead of building walls to block out disturbing realms of the psyche, you are choosing to enter those realms and learn what is there.

As a consequence, your conscious mind may initially struggle with the sudden self-revelations that emerge in dreams. Is this a good thing for your growth? Yes. But is it always pleasant and ego-affirming? No. To make a practice of remembering your dreams is an exercise in radical humility. It teaches you how little you truly know about yourself. Even though Freud was critical of religion and considered himself an atheist, his psychoanalytic ideas still have spiritual relevance today because, at base, he is trying to keep us truly honest about ourselves. We are no less prone to resistance, repression, and self-delusion than were his patients a century ago. Freud remains an indispensable guide for navigating the challenges of a deep, sustained exploration of the dreaming imagination.

Metaphors We Dream By

Still, the uncertainty lingers. If dreams can take so many various forms, and if they can deviate so dramatically from ordinary waking life, how can we be sure they mean anything at all? How do we know they are not just random nonsense from the sleeping brain?

Just about everyone who studies dreams hears this question at some point, and it provides a good opportunity to explore our core beliefs about the meaningfulness of dreams. How would you respond if someone told you dreams are so bizarre and disjointed that trying to interpret them is pointless? Maybe you have already heard someone say that—or wondered it yourself.

Here is Jung's response to this perennial query about whether dreams are simply nonsense: "But if dreams produce such essential compensations, why are they not understandable? I have often been asked this question. The answer must be that the dream is a natural occurrence, and that nature shows no inclination to offer her fruits *gratis* or according to human expectations." Rather than expecting dreams to make sense in the language of the waking mind, Jung suggests the waking mind should try doing more to understand the language of dreaming. Instead of bringing the dream *up*, we bring consciousness *down* so it can learn how dreams express themselves in their native realm. We don't rush to assign a meaning to the dream; we bracket all that out and follow the dream's images and energies wherever they lead. Here again the exploration of dreaming becomes a practice of humility, of suspending the ego's expectations and opening oneself to learning the various ways in which dreams express their meanings. You may find—I cannot guarantee this, but it certainly happens often enough—that once those ego expectations are fully set aside, your intuitive senses will come to the fore, and you will begin to understand things that once seemed impossibly obscure and irrelevant.

An excellent source for this approach is George Lakoff and Mark Johnson's book *Metaphors We Live By*. Their work reveals that dreaming and waking thought are not that different but share a grounding in metaphorical thinking. The essence of metaphor, according to Lakoff and Johnson, is conceiving the *unknown* in terms of the *known*. Whenever we confront something new or unfamiliar in the world, we try to make sense of it in terms of something we already know, something familiar and tangible. For example, say you have just begun a new romantic relationship. Describing it to a friend, you might say it's off to a "fast start," or there might be some "twists and turns ahead," but both of you are "enjoying the ride" and eager to "see where it leads." This illustrates what Lakoff and Johnson call the "love is a journey" metaphor. Love (the *target*, in their terminology) is the new, unfamiliar thing you are trying to understand, and a journey (the *source*) is the familiar, well-known thing you are using to help in that process. You may not have any experience with love, but you do have experience with journeys, and the metaphorical connection between the two facilitates the use of knowledge from one sphere of life to orient you in the other, newer sphere.

The richness and creativity of human thought depends on metaphorical thinking. Each metaphor highlights some aspects of the source while ignoring other aspects. Yes, love is like a journey, but love is also *not* like a journey. It can be metaphorically conceived as a gift, a madness, a chemical reaction—all of which may be true and accurate in highlighting certain aspects of love the other metaphors have missed. Each individual metaphor always downplays or obscures other important features of the source. As Lakoff and Johnson emphasize, we depend on multiple metaphors to guide us through the complexities of life, and the challenge is always how to expand our awareness and understanding through metaphors without letting them become conceptual traps that block us from certain aspects of reality. In this view, metaphors do not simply embroider our regular language as poetic decorations. Rather, we are thinking metaphorically at all times. Much of this occurs unconsciously, so you may not always notice the metaphors in action. But if you take a moment to look around, you will find them everywhere—not just in waking life but in dreams too.

That is where I have been leading with this long detour into Lakoff and Johnson's work. (How's that for an example of the "argument is a journey" metaphor?) In fact, Lakoff wrote an article directly on this topic of metaphors and dream interpretation, where he says that traditional practices of interpretation usually involve identifying metaphorical connections in dreams. As an example, we might think of Pharaoh's dreams in the Bible's book of Genesis, with the seven healthy cows and ears of grain that are consumed by seven sickly and dying cows and ears of grain. Joseph interprets these dreams to mean that seven years of agricultural plenty will be followed by seven years of drought and famine. Because the same basic metaphors appear in two different dreams, Joseph assures the Pharaoh that the interpretation is accurate. Armed with this foreknowledge, the Pharaoh can arrange for extra grain to be stored during the current good times so his people will have food during the coming bad times.

Lakoff's approach emphasizes that waking and dreaming mental activities are both rooted in the same basic processes that unconsciously shape all human thought:

> The metaphor system plays a generative role in dreaming—mediating between the meaning of the dream to the dreamer and what is seen, heard, and otherwise experienced dynamically in the act of dreaming. Given a meaning to be expressed, the metaphor system provides a means of expressing it concretely—in ways that can be seen and heard. That is, the metaphor system, which is in place for waking thought and expression, is

also available during sleep, and provides a natural mechanism for relating concrete images to abstract meanings. The dreamer may well, of course, not be aware, upon waking, of the meaning of the dream since he did not consciously direct the choice of dream imagery to metaphorically express the meaning of the dream.

In this view, dreaming differs from waking thought because dreams can make a wider range of metaphorical connections. The usual constraints on our mental activities disappear when we slumber. During sleep, there is no need to worry about the outer world. The unconscious can create whatever metaphors it likes, without any external hindrances or concerns. For this reason, dreaming can become a primal source of metaphorical creativity, going far beyond the ordinary capabilities of our waking minds.

Expanding on this research, anthropologist Jeannette Mageo has shown how dreams can be analyzed according to three different levels of metaphor: the *universal*, the *personal*, and the *cultural*. The universal level includes metaphors relating to common features of human life found in all places and times. For instance, the metaphors "good is up" and "bad is down" use our ordinary experiences with gravity as sources. These experiences with gravity have instilled within all of us a deep, unconscious connection between good things and an upward direction and between bad things and a downward direction.

By contrast, metaphors at the personal level involve connections relating to specific features of the individual's life, which might make sense to no one else in the world. Thus, someone might have recurrent dreams revolving around a "love is an ice cream cone" metaphor because their first big romance in high school started with a shared ice cream cone. Now that familiar and highly tangible image may serve as a personal dream metaphor to express complex, hard-to-articulate romantic feelings.

Mageo's third type of dream metaphor—the cultural—interests her most as an anthropologist. Here, the metaphorical connection only makes sense within a specific cultural context. If people have dreams involving the metaphor "good is a home run," they probably live in a culture where baseball is a meaningful sporting activity. In America, where baseball is known as the national pastime, this metaphor becomes even more culturally complex and illuminating.

What Does It Look Like in Practice?

This is a question I learned from John McDargh, a true spiritual leader who served for many years as a professor of theology at Boston College. John was a wonderful mentor when I was a graduate student attending my first religious studies conferences, and he introduced me to the community of teachers, scholars, therapists, and clergy who work at the intersection of psychology, culture, and religion. To this day, they remain one of my most cherished group of friends. John once mentioned during a panel discussion that when he is reading a book or an article, he periodically writes "WDLLP?" in the margin: What Does It Look Like in Practice? He does this, he said, to note places where he agrees with the author in principle but wonders if the ideas can be translated into actual reality.

We have now reached a point where John's question may be fairly asked: what does it look like in practice? Let me offer an example of a dream and its interpretation to show how these ideas work in practice and what is involved in identifying metaphors at these different levels. For this initial foray into actual dreams, I have chosen one of my own recent dreams. Other examples in the book will involve big dreams of various kinds from people other than myself. Here my hope is to highlight, in their simplest forms, the appearance of various kinds of metaphors in dreams. By doing so, I hope to prepare us for deeper explorations.

Bernard Says, "Run"

The dream occurred about two weeks prior to this writing, so it remains fresh in my mind as I reflect on it. The dream happened during one of the nights a group of friends stayed with me as visitors in my home near Portland, Oregon. We had all just attended the annual conference of the International Association for the Study of Dreams, and now we had gathered for a few days to debrief in a calmer, quieter setting. My friend Bernard was among them, and he was the key character in this dream.

> We are in a room, with lots of people. . . . The room starts spinning clockwise, like a merry-go-round. . . . We all start stumbling and losing our balance as the spinning accelerates. . . . But Bernard has his balance, and he simply says, "Run". . . . What?. . . . "Run" is all he says. . . . I do, and I realize I can go around the spinning room fine, running counterclockwise and thus keeping my balance, moving as I will. . . . The other people, though, are in a clump, lost to the momentum of the room, unable to control their bodies. . . . It's like a weird Twister game. . . . Finally, I say to Bernard, "Tell us your secret, so we know how it is we can all keep our balance here."

Bernard and I have known each other for more than twenty years, and he is one of the people I most respect in the world of dream research. In 2011, we coauthored a book with Philip King titled *Dreaming in the Classroom*, about methods and practices in teaching students about dreams in various educational settings. Bernard has amazing expertise in film, poetry, theater, and the humanities in general, and he knows as much as any psychologist about current scientific advances in dream research. I have always encouraged him to find new ways to share his knowledge, especially through writing, which he does very well but, by his own admission, very slowly.

Those are the first associations that come to mind in relation to the dream's waking context. Now let's consider the metaphors in the dream, using Mageo's three-part approach as a guide.

As a universal human phenomenon, the gravitational polarity of *up* versus *down* seems important in the dream. I try hard to stay on my feet, and I do not want to fall down like the others. So the dream features the metaphors "good is up" and "bad is down" but with a twist (so to speak). The factor of *motion* is added to the up-down dynamic, transforming the polarity into one of *balance* versus *imbalance*: "good is balance" and "bad is imbalance."

As a personal metaphor, the character of Bernard represents several meanings that are distinctive to my perception of him in waking life. His appearance in this dream foregrounds my respect for his knowledge about important topics that few other people fully appreciate. He remains up and balanced in the dream, while everyone else has fallen down. And his helpful behavior in the dream—delivering eloquent, effective advice with a trickster's smile and a twinkle in his eye—matches what I have seen when he is on a roll in waking life and making good points in a lecture or discussion. I suspect most other people who know Bernard have noticed this quality too. In this dream, then, I see a very specific personal metaphor: "Knowledge is Bernard." Do what he says, and I can stay up and maintain my balance.

At least two elements in the dream seem to be cultural metaphors: the merry-go-round and the reference to the game of Twister. Most people who grew up in my cultural environment (middle-class American suburbs in the 1960s and 1970s) would be familiar with merry-go-rounds and Twister and would immediately recognize their metaphorical possibilities. If you did not have this cultural background, however, these references would make little sense without some further description. Twister is an acrobatic party game in which people take turns placing their hands and feet on the colored dots of a big square floor mat; as the game progresses, people become increasingly contorted around and on top of each other, and whoever falls down first loses. Merry-go-rounds were standard features of amusement parks at the time, with a variety of fabricated show horses and circus animals to sit upon and ride around.

With that background, what could be the metaphorical meaning of these two cultural references? In perhaps the simplest terms, they both transform what could be a frightening situation of physical vulnerability into something fun: a children's game, a form of play. People spinning out of control and falling down in a tangle of limbs—that's not a titanic nightmare; it's like a game of Twister or like riding the merry-go-round. And within the space of that playful dynamic, Bernard's one-word imperative—*run*—comes across less like the title of a Jordan Peele horror movie and more like an amusing bit of wordplay. The cultural metaphor at work here might be phrased as "life is a game of movement."

Drawing these three levels of metaphor together, we could say the dream uses familiar things in my waking life (physical balance and gravity, Bernard, merry-go-rounds, and Twister) to help make sense of questions and concerns that are less familiar and more abstract (the good, knowledge, life). That's only a partial interpretation, though. A full interpretation would go on to ask why *those* specific questions and concerns emerged in *this* specific dream at *this* specific time in my life.

In later chapters, we will discuss several other methods of dream interpretation, almost all of which become more powerful and effective when combined with metaphor analysis. For now, we can note that metaphors in dreaming differ from metaphors in waking because they are *embodied*, not just conceptual or cognitive in nature. In my dream, I did not just *think* "good is balance"; I *felt* and *experienced* this as a vivid, physical sensation. As the room spun around and I gradually figured out how to do as Bernard suggested—run in the opposite direction from the spin—the dream metaphor became a living, embodied reality. Metaphors in dreaming are not only more varied than in waking; they can be more experientially intense too.

Getting It Wrong

The corollary of the difficulty of interpreting dreams is the ease of misinterpreting dreams. Just as we should be suspicious of those who are overly hasty in dismissing dreams as meaningless, we should also keep a skeptical eye on those who claim with instant certainty what the meaning of a particular dream is. The first idea that pops into your mind about a dream may be a valuable "aha!" discovery, but it may also be a defensive maneuver to avoid confronting other possible meanings in the dream. Here again, an intentional practice of humility can help to set aside the expectations of your waking ego and learn what the non-ego parts of your psyche are trying to say. Curiosity, openness, a willingness to be surprised—these are the cardinal virtues of dream interpretation. With them, virtually any dream, big or little, can yield interesting insights into your life and the world. Without them, you can end up trapped in a roomful of mirrors.

A simple practice to elude this trap is called bias control. It comes from psychologist Eugene Gendlin in his book *Let Your Body Interpret Your Dreams*. After reflecting on your dream for a while and reaching a point where you think you have a good idea about what it means, pause for a moment and try thinking of the exact *opposite* meaning for the dream and see how that feels. For instance, if your dream seems to be about your anger at a friend, stop to consider the possibility that the dream is also about how much you care for your friend. If your dream seems focused on death and destruction, imagine for a moment it's also a dream about life and rebirth. If your dream appears to express a romantic interest in someone, think of how the dream might also express a nonromantic connection with that person. Just let the contrary idea dwell in your mind for a moment. Maybe it's not relevant and just leads to a dead end. But maybe it opens up new feelings and insights you would not have noticed otherwise. The practice of bias control gives you an easy way to test your interpretations and check if you might be missing something important.

CHAPTER 3

More than Therapy
Sharing Dreams

I first met Jeremy Taylor in the summer of 1987. My mother and his wife, Kathy, knew each other from their studies and work at San Francisco Theological Seminary in San Anselmo, California. At some point, they realized Jeremy and I were both interested in dreams. I had just finished the first year of a PhD program in religion and psychology, with a focus on dreaming, and Jeremy was a Unitarian-Universalist minister who led dream-sharing groups. He invited me to his house in San Rafael for an initial chat and then asked if I would like to attend a session of the dream-sharing group he facilitated at the San Gregorio Community Center, in a quiet, woodsy corner of the Bay Area.

The experience was life-changing. I had previously participated in a few dream discussion groups, but never had I been part of a process that so powerfully energized every single member of the group. It felt synergistic, like the whole of our group dynamic became much more than the sum of our individual perspectives. "Because dreams always merge many levels of meaning into a single metaphor of dream experience, it is almost always productive to share dreams with people you care about and ask them about their dreams," Taylor writes in his breakthrough book *Dream Work.* "When the multiple intelligences and intuitions of several people are brought to bear on a dream or series of dreams, it is much more likely that the dreamer will be exposed to a fuller range of the dream's possible meaning, and will have a chance to 'tingle' and resonate with a wider spectrum of the dream's multiple levels and layers of significance."

Other therapists have developed good methods for sharing dreams, and I will discuss some of those approaches later in the chapter, but Jeremy was the first to teach me about the deep potential of a group process of dream-sharing. I know he has had a similar impact on the countless other people who met and worked with him during his more than forty years of virtually nonstop traveling, teaching, counseling, and writing. When I think of what a spiritual leader looks like, Jeremy Taylor quickly comes to mind.

Dream-sharing is a natural outgrowth of interpreting dreams, and it's an important step in the process of transforming individual dreams into calls for collective change. We will look in this chapter at several historical examples of dreams that helped people in moments of crisis for their communities—such as Indigenous people of the Americas defending their cultures against White settlers, and Black people fleeing slavery and fighting for racial justice. Dream-sharing is not a magic wand that can stop horrible things from happening. But it is a powerful and resilient tool for endangered, crisis-stricken groups to communicate their feelings, preserve their most important values, and spark practical actions for social change and cultural transformation.

Maybe You Shouldn't

Perhaps you feel some hesitancy around the idea of sharing your dreams with other people. If so, that is perfectly natural. Your dreams express something very important and personal about your life, and of course you don't want to share that with just anyone.

This natural wariness hardens into strict boundaries in modern Western society, where subtle but unmistakable limits are set around when, where, why, and with whom you can share your dreams. A client with a therapist, a child with a parent, a participant in a research study, a close friend in the corner of a party—that about sums up the situations in which it would be considered socially acceptable to share a dream. In general, it would *not* be considered socially acceptable to share dreams at work, for example, or during a college class, in a religious worship service, at the grocery store, or in a political meeting.

If you were to violate the implicit social code and share a dream in one of these off-limits spaces, you would likely be met with strange looks and dismissive comments about dreams. And if someone really wanted to put you in your place, they'd tell you that hearing other people tell their dreams is *boring*—and not just regular boring but painfully boring, unbearably boring, in fact one of the most boring things one person can do to another. Perhaps you have never been on the receiving end of this particular critique of dreaming, but those who have experienced this response when they have shared a dream know that it carries a special vehemence and hostility. People may say they feel "bored" by another's dreams, but their reactions convey much more active, if also unconscious, energy than that. According to survey research I have done with my colleague Michael Schredl, an empirical psychologist in Germany, about a quarter of the US adult population agrees with the idea that listening to other people's dreams is boring. This is sobering evidence of modern society's reflexive bias against and defensiveness toward anything having to do with dreaming.

To share your dreams with someone else, then, not only means overcoming your general caution about personal disclosure. It means accepting the one-in-four chance that the other person will have no interest in what you say.

It's also not unheard of for people to take another's dreams *so* seriously that they attack the dreamer. That's what Joseph's brothers did when they tried to rid themselves of the threatening dreams of their younger sibling. This is what the witch-hunting inquisitors did as well when they tried to silence medieval women who articulated inexplicable knowledge and uncanny dreams of flying. This is what the opponents of the Rev. Martin Luther King Jr. tried to do to destroy his radical dream of overcoming racism, poverty, and war. King's use of the term in the "I Have a Dream" speech at the Lincoln Memorial on August 28, 1963, is primarily metaphorical. But there is evidence that an actual dream influenced him significantly on at least one occasion. We will look more closely at his experience later in this chapter.

Another challenge of dream-sharing is the possibility that another person is making up their dreams and using them to manipulate others. What if they are lying and fabricating stories presented as dreams? You know when *you* are telling the truth about your own dreams, but how can you be sure someone else is doing the same? This dangerous uncertainty prompted the biblical prophet Jeremiah to warn people against false visionaries who make grandiose religious claims based only on the evidence of their personal dreams. In this passage, he speaks on behalf of

God against those who seek attention because of their divine dreaming:

> I have heard what the prophets have said who prophesy lies in my name, saying, "I have dreamed! I have dreamed!" How long shall there be lies in the heart of the prophets who prophesy lies, and who prophesy the deceit of their own heart, who think to make my people forget my name by their dreams which they tell one another, even as their fathers forgot my name for Ba'al? Let the prophet who has a dream tell the dream, but let him who has my word speak my word faithfully. What has straw in common with wheat? (Jer 23:25–28 RSV)

Jeremiah makes the same basic point two more times, in chapters 27 and 29, which underscores the importance of his warning and suggests he was addressing a real problem at the time. In this early period of its history, Judaism was a relatively small and tenuous faith community. Jeremiah and his fellow Jews were trying to hold their own against many other large and powerful religious traditions, most of which regarded dreams as one of the primary means by which humans interact with the gods. Jeremiah raised his alarm in this context, at a time when the spiritual currency of dreaming was being undermined by counterfeiters. To be clear, Jeremiah did not reject dreaming or the sharing of dreams; "let the prophet who has a dream tell the dream," he said. Rather, he wanted people to exercise more critical caution toward prophetic claims of God-inspired dreaming, to be more careful about the distinction between dreams of the divine and dreams from one's own heart. Just because someone had a powerful dream that's true and revelatory for *them* doesn't mean the dream is true and revelatory for *you*. A dream from one's own heart can be a legitimate and wonderful gift with deep personal meaning, but that alone does not qualify it as a heaven-sent vision of divine significance.

Alas, the solution to one problem too often begets another. You may have already anticipated where this can lead. Jeremiah's skepticism, carried to its logical conclusion, ultimately casts doubt on *all* dreams. How can we *ever* know if a person is lying or telling the truth when sharing a dream? This inability to verify another person's dream can make everything about dreaming appear uncertain, suspicious, and ripe for abuse.

And regarding your own dreams: How certain can you feel, really, that you understand what they mean? That you can translate their metaphors and images into the language your conscious brain understands? That you can accurately distinguish the wishes of your own heart from a direct message from God? In light of all these challenges inherent in interpreting and sharing our dreams, it might seem wisest to ignore dreams entirely. Why waste time on something that's complicated at best and misleading at worst?

Once again, we see how cultural teachings and personal anxieties can combine to discourage people from paying attention to their dreams. Jeremiah's cautionary words have merit and should be taken seriously. But we need more than his pointed skepticism to guide us forward. How can we avoid the trap of rejecting all dreams just because some of them are difficult to understand or because other people misuse theirs?

From Inner Experience to Living Culture

The early-twentieth-century theories of Freud and Jung are still a huge influence on modern attitudes toward dreaming. In Freud's memorable phrase, "the interpretation of dreams is the *via regia* (royal road) to a knowledge of the unconscious parts of the mind." Both Freud and Jung interpreted the dreams of their clients as a regular part of therapy. Yet neither of them encouraged ordinary people to delve into their dreams outside of a therapeutic context. On the contrary, they emphasized that dream interpretation requires specialized knowledge in psychiatry, history, comparative mythology, and folklore. They warned against the dangers of suddenly encountering energies from the unconscious without preparation or guidance.

We can agree with Freud and Jung about the value of specialized knowledge without agreeing that such information is *required* for interpreting a dream. Likewise, we can accept their cautionary words about surprises from the unconscious but still reject the implication that dreams should *never* be interpreted outside the presence of a professional expert. Humans have been dreaming, sharing their dreams, and interpreting them together since time immemorial—long before the appearance of Western psychology. Whatever is *required* for interpreting dreams, we must already possess those qualities within us, at least in their potential form. Deep down, we know how to share and interpret dreams; we just don't always *know* that we know.

To be clear, interpreting dreams in a therapeutic setting can be incredibly helpful. Especially during times of crisis and suffering, when therapy may be required, dreams can provide strong resources for the healing process. But dreaming is not itself a therapeutic object or phenomenon, and it cannot be defined solely in terms of its role in therapy. Dreaming is a natural, normal, healthy expression of the human psyche, a powerful gift within the mind of every individual, manifesting itself in various ways throughout the life cycle.

Most cultures around the world contain practices for sharing and interpreting dreams. In fact, anthropologists consider dream interpretation to be a cultural universal, found in some form or another among all human communities. The following examples give a sense of this bigger picture. The Yansi people of central Africa, as anthropologist Mubuy Mubay Mpier observes, seek dreams and discuss their meanings in relation to important group activities such as hunting, going on a journey, and performing a ritual. When twins are born, the Yansi perform a special rite, the exact timing of which is determined after the village elders have slept outside under the stars and then gathered in the morning to discuss their dreams. Their group interpretations focus on trying to discern the attitudes of their dead ancestors toward the planned ritual since their participation is considered essential to the ceremony's ultimate success.

For the Xavante people of the central Brazilian plateau, dream-sharing of a special kind plays a central role in male initiation rituals. The transition from boyhood into manhood involves contacting the ancestors through dreaming and receiving from them one's own *da-nore*, or "dream song." According to anthropologist Laura Graham, when a young male initiate has a dream in which the ancestral spirits sing his special song for him, he must do his utmost to remember it and then share it with the group. As all the initiates share their individual *da-nore*, a new collective dream emerges. What began as an expression of inner experience becomes part of the living culture of the community.

In Australia's Western Desert, the Kukatja Aboriginal people share dreams in ceremonial settings and also as part of ordinary daily life among family members. Anthropologist Sylvie Poirier notes the effectiveness of dream-sharing as a part of Kukatja cultural education: "As a general rule, learning to deal positively and creatively with one's dream experiences is something that the elders try to foster among the young," she writes. "The Kukatja world is filled with malevolent spirits, vengeful sorcerers, and powerful ancestral beings who can also all be encountered in dreams. Learning to be able to meet these beings face-to-face, either in dreams or in waking life, but also learning to deal positively with one's fears, is surely an important aspect in the process of socialization among the Kukatja."

A few common themes emerge from examples like these. First, dream-sharing tends to occur among people who have a special bond or relationship, like family members or other participants in a ritual. It is an intimate form of communication, not necessarily something one does with strangers. Second, older people play an important role in preserving traditional dream teachings and passing them along to new generations. It may not be a requirement for interpreting dreams, but being an elder and having many years of lived experience seems to strengthen a person's abilities to apprehend the deepest and subtlest patterns of dreaming. Third, dream-sharing often serves as a potent resource in spiritual practices, especially those revolving around death and the dead. As we will discuss in more detail in later chapters, many religious traditions have recognized a close connection between sleep, dreams, and death. These traditions put extra emphasis on sharing "visitation dreams," dreams of someone who has died appearing as if they are alive again. Such dreams are among the most widely experienced types of spiritually transformative big dreams, with meanings that extend beyond a purely personal sphere of reference.

This leads to the fourth theme in these cross-cultural practices of dream-sharing: They aim to elicit meanings not only for the individual dreamer but for the community too. Unlike standard practices of modern psychotherapy, which focus on dreams strictly in relation to an individual's personal concerns and problems, many cultural groups around the world also look to dreams for insights about collective concerns and problems. The healing dynamics are essentially the same, just applied at different scales.

Sharing Dreams for Cultural Survival

A harrowing example of dream-sharing as a collective resource can be found in the so-called Dreamer religions of nineteenth-century Native American communities. These groups were struggling against violent attacks and encroachment of White settlers, led by the US Army. The term *Dreamer religions* was first used by US government officials as a negative term for a variety of dream-related spiritual activities among the Native Americans that the officials regarded as ignorant, superstitious, politically subversive, and anti-Christian. Ironically, these officials were right about the key cultural role of dreams for the Native communities during this time of horrific crisis. And although they could only see it through their own narrow, biased framework, the US officials also recognized that in dreaming, the Native groups were finding a genuine source of resistance and resilience.

What was actually happening with these new dream-centered spiritual movements among the Native groups at this time? The story of Smohalla, a member of the Wanapum community of the Pacific Northwest, can illustrate. Smohalla was well known among his people as a healer, cultural leader, and prophet. During the years 1858–1860, Native groups all across the Columbia River plateau suffered a series of catastrophic defeats in battles against the US Army. At one point, Smohalla and a small group of his family and followers retreated to a remote area, where they stopped to care for his young daughter, who had fallen ill during their anxious, rushed travels. Smohalla had been training her from an early age as his successor and preparing her for her vision quest. Yet now all his medicines were proving useless; he could not save her. After the girl passed away, Smohalla spent a long time sitting at her grave, praying, singing, and mourning her loss.

During this period of intense grief, he experienced a powerful dream-vision: He died and ascended to the spirit world, where he was taught a series of sacred dances and songs. These ritual practices were revealed to him so he could bring them to his people to help them stay connected to the traditional ways of their ancestors. When Smohalla finally awoke, he shared the dances and songs with the group, who immediately recognized the value of his dream not only for his personal healing but for the healing of the whole community. A ceremony was soon organized to perform these dances and songs, and a new burst of interest in their oldest spiritual traditions took hold of the community. By sharing his dream with others during a time of collective crisis, Smohalla helped to renew and reinvigorate their deepest cultural bonds with each other.

In a different part of nineteenth-century America, another brutally violent assault on community survival was being waged. Enslaved Black people, who had been brought against their will from various parts of Africa, struggled not only to stay alive but also to preserve their most precious spiritual and cultural teachings while forced to dwell in a hostile, alien land. One of the most important of these African spiritual traditions involved the prophetic power of dreaming. Everyone in the community was encouraged to listen to their dreams for possible insights into the future, especially in times of great uncertainty and danger. Of those who suffered and yet lived through the horrors of this era, the most vivid dreamer known to history is Harriet Tubman. Tubman, who gained great fame as a heroic leader of the Underground Railroad, personally led dozens of enslaved Black people on the long and extremely dangerous journey from the South to states in the North. What is less known is the role of dreaming and dream-sharing in her fight to save her people and forge a better future for the whole community.

Born into slavery in 1822, Tubman was frequently beaten as a child. At one point, a White man threw a large piece of metal and struck her in the head, dealing a grievous blow that was never medically treated. From that point onward, Harriet experienced a variety of unusual spiritual phenomena, including extremely powerful dreams. Once she dreamed she was flying, soaring high in the sky like a bird, passing over landscapes she did not recognize. The dream gave her a feeling of strength and confidence, which was likely bolstered by traditional African beliefs about flying dreams as good fortunes and symbols of spiritual power. Only later did she recognize that this flying dream had given her a prophetic glimpse of what lay ahead in her efforts to escape to the North and gain freedom for herself and her people. She also had frequent dreams of striving to escape, facing harsh obstacles, becoming too weak to go on, and then receiving a helping hand from others willing to aid in pulling her across. According to historian Mechal Sobel, in her thought-provoking book about dreams in American history, *Teach Me Dreams*, Tubman followed these dreams when she finally did reach the North and appealed to White abolitionists to support her. For years, she led daring rescue missions, secretly traveling back and forth into slave-holding territories and ultimately liberating dozens of people. Sobel comments, "It was her use of dreams and visions that enabled her to become a leader among both black men and women, one who had a price on her head in the South, at the same time that she was sought as a partner by white abolitionists in the North." For Harriet Tubman, dreaming and sharing dreams served as a kind of spiritual compass that gave her a strong sense of confidence in her direction and a clear awareness of the challenges and opportunities ahead.

The Vision in the Kitchen

Late one night in January 1956, civil rights leader Martin Luther King Jr. received a phone call just before falling asleep. It was another angry, hate-filled voice telling him to get out of Montgomery. The twenty-five-year-old King was the new minister of the Dexter Avenue Baptist Church, and he had recently become a leader of the public bus boycott sparked by the refusal of Rosa Parks to give up her seat for a White passenger. King had been receiving constant threats of violence since the boycott began, and after putting the phone down from this particular call, he could not go back to sleep.

As he recounts in his 1958 book, *Stride toward Freedom*, King suddenly felt overwhelmed by his fears and all the pressures of trying to lead his community through a time of extreme crisis. While the rest of his family slept, he paced through the house for a while. Then he went to the kitchen to make a pot of coffee and sat down at the table:

> I was ready to give up. With my cup of coffee sitting untouched before me I tried to think of a way to move out of the picture without appearing a coward. In this state of exhaustion, when my courage had all but gone, I decided to take my problem to God. With my head in

my hands, I bowed over the kitchen table and prayed aloud. The words I spoke to God that midnight are still vivid in my memory. "I am here taking a stand for what I believe is right. But now I am afraid. The people are looking to me for leadership, and if I stand before them without strength and courage, they too will falter. I am at the end of my powers. I have nothing left. I've come to the point where I can't face it alone." At that moment I experienced the presence of the Divine as I had never experienced Him before. It seemed as though I could hear the quiet assurance of an inner voice saying, "Stand up for righteousness, stand up for truth; and God will be at your side forever." Almost at once my fears began to go. My uncertainty disappeared and I was ready to face anything.

In her commentary on King's experience, dream researcher Patricia M. Davis observes that his divine revelation takes an auditory rather than visual form, although King himself refers to it as a vision. He does not specifically say it was a dream, but all the details of his condition at that moment suggest that, at the least, he entered a dreamlike state of consciousness. It was late at night, he was alone, he didn't drink the coffee, his head was down, his ego had given up, and he opened his mind to God—and then he hears an autonomous voice delivering a message of heavenly reassurance. As Davis notes, "He seems to be deliberately leaving open the possibility that he had dozed off."

Three days after this experience, a bomb exploded on the front porch of King's home. Fortunately, he and the family were not home. But the murderous intention was clear. And yet King did not pull back from his leadership of the Montgomery bus boycott; instead, he pushed it forward for another grueling year, persuading people to persist in their nonviolent protests, until the US Supreme Court ruled in late 1956 that racially segregated buses were unconstitutional.

Soon after the Supreme Court decision, King gave a sermon in which he mentioned for the first time in public what happened in his kitchen almost a year earlier. The *Montgomery Advertiser* newspaper gave the following report of the sermon:

> The Rev. Martin Luther King, Jr. told his congregation yesterday that he had a vision early one morning a year ago telling him to lead the Montgomery Negro Movement against segregation without fear . . . King said in prayer: "I realize that there were moments when I wanted to give up and I was afraid but You gave me a vision in the kitchen of my house and I am thankful for it. . . . Early on a sleepless morning in January 1956," King said, "rationality left me." Then, "almost out of nowhere I heard a voice that morning saying to me: 'Preach the Gospel, stand up for truth, stand up for righteousness.'" King went on, "Since that morning I can stand up without fear. So I'm not afraid of anybody this morning. Tell Montgomery they can keep shooting and I'm going to stand up to them."

This courageous and inspiring sense of fearlessness, which characterized King's civil rights work for the rest of his life, had its roots in a personal experience of spiritual dreaming. He shared the story of his "vision in the kitchen" several times over the years, always emphasizing the powerful impact of those vivid words. It seems likely that this divine reassurance was in his mind when he stood before hundreds of thousands of people at the Lincoln Memorial in Washington, DC, on August 28,

1963, and said these words: "I say to you today, my friends, so even though we face the difficulties of today and tomorrow, I still have a dream. It is a dream deeply rooted in the American dream. I have a dream that one day this nation will rise up and live out the true meaning of its creed: 'We hold these truths to be self-evident: that all men are created equal.'"

By sharing his prophetic dream of social justice with a massive crowd at one of the most hallowed civic spaces in the nation, King successfully aligned his personal vision with a collective vision of the ultimate equality of all people. He appealed to the capacity for spiritual dreaming in everyone as something that binds us together and can give us guidance as we strive to make his dream—and God's dream—a reality.

A Method for Group Dream-Sharing

Dream-sharing in many cultures tends to be carefully limited to people who are close to each other and deeply familiar with a shared way of life. Those conditions do not always apply in present-day Western society, where we interact constantly with large numbers of unfamiliar people from a wide variety of different backgrounds. The dream-sharing techniques developed in traditional cultures can be helpful, but modern Westerners need something that can be helpful with our specifically *mul-ti*cultural circumstances. We need an approach that addresses a relatively novel situation in the history of dreaming: how can we enable a group of relative strangers to share and discuss their dreams together?

This background helps us understand better what Jeremy Taylor and Montague Ullman were doing when they both developed, independent of each other, a modern practice for group dream-sharing. Both Taylor and Ullman knew about anthropological studies of dream-sharing, and they both recognized that Western psychological approaches to dreams were limited by their exclusive focus on the individual. Their methods for dream-sharing developed with the intention of bringing the energies of dreams more fully into communities, into a collective sphere of meaning and healing impact. In this way, they tried to realign contemporary dreamwork with the practices of cultures in which dream-sharing is a natural, normal part of community life, with benefits for both the individual dreamer and the group as a whole.

In other ways, however, the method developed by Taylor and Ullman has no historical or cross-cultural precedent and actually represents a uniquely modern approach to dreaming. It reflects contemporary Western attitudes and ideals that not everyone shares, but it still may contribute something new and valuable to humanity's general understanding of dreams. (The same might be true of lucid dreaming in the West; we'll get to that in chapter 7.) People sometimes ask me if other cultures share dreams the same way we do when we use Taylor and Ullman's approach, and to the best of my knowledge, the answer is no. It seems this way of sharing dreams only emerged in the specific cultural circumstances of the latter part of the twentieth century in the United States and Western Europe. In what follows, I will focus on Taylor since I knew him better and have more experience with the nuances of his approach. Almost everything that follows has its corresponding place in Ullman's system, however—a framework I highly recommend as well.

Taylor's efforts in this area began in the late 1960s in northern California. After registering as a conscientious objector and refusing to serve as a soldier in the Vietnam War, he was assigned to do alternative service. During these years, he did organizing work in Oakland, Emeryville, and other parts of the East Bay. After long and fruitless efforts to build bridges across communities of racial, ethnic, and economic difference, he stumbled across the practice of dream-sharing. He found that encouraging people to talk about dreams enabled them to discuss deep emotional concerns and painful waking-life experiences in a relatively indirect and nonconfrontational way. It did not take him long to realize how powerful this method could be: "It seems clear that leaderless and lay-led group dream work may eventually become a vital factor in promoting community mental health," he wrote.

Taylor's approach can be easily summarized, although of course no written description can fully convey the experience of participating in a dream-sharing group. Basically, everyone in the dream-sharing group should sit comfortably in a circle, and the setting should be quiet and private enough to prevent distractions or concerns about safety and confidentiality. Once the group gathers (it can be as few as three people or as many as a dozen or more), the first few moments are devoted to checking in, letting everyone say something brief about how they're feeling or what's going on in their lives. After that, a centering exercise of quiet, slow breathing with the eyes closed allows the group to settle down, bracket out the rest of the world, and focus their best intuitive energies on the dreams to be shared. The typical process, then, is for each member of the group to go around the circle and share a dream. At this point, only the dream is shared—no background, no associations, no extra commentary. Just the dream.

Whenever people share their dreams, Taylor encourages them to use the present tense, not the past tense, in the description. Using the present tense has the effect of making the dream feel more alive and immediate, which is an essential feature of Taylor's method. Compare these two versions of the same dream image:

> "I opened a door and saw a big dog, who jumped up and growled at me."
> "I open a door and see a big dog, who jumps up and growls at me."

They both describe the same scene, but the latter comes across as livelier and more immersive, like it is happening right here and now. Indeed, that is precisely the goal: to enable each member of the group to form their own vivid, actively imagined version of the dream within their own minds. Using the present tense makes it much easier to achieve that goal.

Each meeting of the group may only allow for a full discussion of one or two dreams, so it is important at the outset to give everyone a chance to share some dream energy and imagery with the group. In the interests of time, it might make sense for each person just to share a title of a dream, not the whole thing. Once everyone has shared at least a portion or a title of a dream, the group decides to focus on one dream in particular. Perhaps the group has decided to take turns, or maybe someone has volunteered to share, or perhaps someone in the group has shared a particularly unusual dream that everyone is eager to explore. As long as each member knows they will get a chance for the group to focus on their dream in this session or an upcoming one, serendipity can lead the way to choosing a dream for special attention.

The dreamer is now invited to share the dream again, in the present tense. If the person read the dream verbatim from a journal the first time, now I would ask them to put the journal down, close their eyes, and share the dream from memory. In most cases, this will enhance the feeling among the whole group of entering more fully into their imagined versions of the dream. Inevitably, there will be discrepancies between the individual's two recitations of the dream, and that is okay; slight variations in the narrative can open interesting paths of meaning.

After the second telling, members of the group ask the dreamer questions of clarification, such as "Is it night or day in the dream?" or "What color is the big dog?" or "How do you feel when the dog growls at you?" Sometimes the dreamer has a clear answer to these questions, and sometimes the dream itself is vague on a certain point. At this stage of the process, it's less helpful to ask for personal associations that shift the group's focus to something other than the dream. Questions like "Did you have a dog when you were a child?" or "Is there anyone who acts like a growling dog in your waking life?" are legitimate and potentially insightful, but they tend to lead the discussion *away* from the dream itself and its living imagery. Better to bracket out such questions for now and to concentrate on questions that help each member of the group form a clear and distinct version of the dream in their own minds.

Now the dreamer sits back and listens as the others offer their thoughts and impressions about the dream's multiple dimensions of possible meaning. The comments of the group can relate to specific details of the dream, specific scenes or characters, or offer an overarching perspective on the themes in the dream. The group method begins to show its value at this moment. Taylor writes, "One of the reasons why group dream work is so rewarding is that the different ideas, projections, and intuitions of group members are likely to touch a much wider range of possible meaning than can easily be reached working alone or with only one other person." By design, the process becomes open-ended as everyone contributes thoughts and reflections.

But no matter where the discussion leads, Taylor insists that everyone preface their comments with words to the effect of "If it were my dream . . ." Using this preface is important for two reasons. First, it protects the dreamer from intrusive, judgmental comments from group members who may not intend to impose their views on the dreamer but do so anyway. Again, compare the two ways of expressing the same comment:

> "The big growling dog means that someone who is usually loyal to you is now threatening you."
> "If it were my dream, the big growling dog would mean that someone who is usually loyal to me is now threatening me."

The former statement puts an uncomfortable burden on the dreamer to accept or reject the interpretation. Pressure like that does not help the flow of the dream-sharing process. The latter statement, however, gives the dreamer the space to consider whether this interpretation applies to their experience of the dream. It's ultimately a matter of respecting the dreamer and being careful not to impose external meanings on their dream. Members of the group can suggest possible meanings, and that can be enormously helpful, but in the end, it is always up to the dreamer to decide if a particular interpretation makes sense or not.

The second reason for using the "if it were my dream" preface goes to what we might call the metapsychology of Taylor's approach to dreaming. Starting with this phrase when commenting on someone else's dream is not only more polite; it is more accurate. It is simply a better statement of the true state of affairs when we share dreams with each other. The fact is we never have direct access to another person's dream. We only have a reimagined version of the dream within our own minds. That might seem to block us from ever saying anything objectively useful, but it actually liberates our powers of intuition and makes our comments potentially more helpful to the dreamer. Because all humans have the same innate psychological structures and tendencies—what Jung referred to as the "collective unconscious"—one person's dreams can legitimately spark something new and meaningful within the mind of another person in the group, who has a big "aha!" experience as a result. This person's strong response may not be relevant to the dreamer's original experience of the dream— but then again, maybe it is. As each member of the group shares their own "if it were my dream" insights, the dreamer is given the opportunity to consider various perspectives on the dream without any pressure to agree with any of them.

The discussion can proceed as long as the dreamer finds it helpful. At some point, the dreamer will usually hit a limit where they have received enough input for now and would like to conclude the process. Everyone in the group is given a chance to offer a final thought, often of a practical nature (e.g., "If this were my dream, I'd go to a dog park tomorrow and watch the dogs play with each other"). Then the last word goes to the dreamer, who can end the discussion on whatever note they choose. The whole process can take fifteen minutes, or it can take two hours. There is no automatic, official endpoint; it's a matter of the dreamer's engagement, the endurance of the group, and the time limits on the space or people's schedules.

Taylor's method creates a paradoxical dynamic in which the dreamer is best served by everyone else in the group behaving selfishly: that is, taking the dreamer's dream and imagining it as their own. The group helps the dreamer *not* by trying to help the dreamer but by going as deeply as possible into their *own* reimagined version of the dream. They say what the dream means for them as if the dreamer were not even there. Taylor's "if it were my dream" preface stimulates the intuition and imaginative creativity of each group member, enabling them to tap into the collective unconscious and share what comes up for them. And yet the dreamer is always in charge of the process; the group's role is to project their imaginations into the dream and share whatever thoughts and feelings arise for them.

I have taught this method of dream-sharing many times over the years, and it usually takes only a session or two for everyone in the group to get the hang of it. Once, however, my standard lesson plan did not work.

Self-Reflection as a Means of Interpretation

The group members were ministerial students at a Protestant seminary, taking a one-week intensive class with me on dreams in pastoral care and counseling. They were bright, enthusiastic, well-read, deeply religious, and extremely compassionate. But they could not, for the life of them, adopt an "if it were my dream" perspective toward another person's dream. They recognized and appreciated the value of dreams; that wasn't the issue. Rather, it was my emphasis on *self*-reflection as an integral part of the process that tripped them up.

We took a complete timeout from the regular lesson-plan of the class so we could step back and talk about what was happening. It emerged that their theological and pastoral training as ministers-to-be had put so much emphasis on caring for others that it felt like a violation of their calling to reflect, even if only for a moment, on their *own* feelings, thoughts, and intuitions when hearing another person share a dream. They wanted to help the dreamer immediately, directly, and unselfishly, and they were much less prepared to inquire into their own interior lives. I tried different ways of explaining the importance of personally reflecting on concepts like the unconscious, projection, and hidden bias, but to little effect. We made it through the week, but I'm not really sure if I succeeded in the learning objectives of the class. At a minimum, I hope I planted the seeds of some new ideas about dreams. How those ideas grow and develop in the students' minds, I'll never know, but I trust that their dreaming imaginations will make use of what they need.

Once people learn how the process of dream-sharing works, they often find it surprisingly interesting, illuminating, and enjoyable. Thanks to the dedicated efforts of Taylor and many others who have been teaching these methods for several decades now, millions of people have learned how to share and explore their dreams in a group setting. By providing a framework for dream-sharing that is open to all comers, this practice opens up dreamwork to people from whatever background, with no prior experience required. Indeed, the brilliance of the approach is to transform a group of strangers into a unique resource for deeper dream exploration. Cultural pluralism becomes an invaluable ally and a powerful resource for collective discovery. The more diversity among the members of the group, the further everyone can go in their dream explorations.

You could stop here, do nothing more than what these first three chapters have suggested, and your dreams would likely begin to change in dramatic and unexpected ways. The chapters in part I have provided you with a grounding in the simplest and most effective practices for cultivating the spiritual power of your dreams. By paying close attention to the quality of your sleep, actively exploring the metaphorical meanings of your dreams, and sharing dreams with other people in mutually respectful ways, you are essentially putting out the welcome mat for your dreaming imagination. Who or what will respond to your invitation? How exactly will your dreams change? What will they reveal? Where will they take you? We turn now to three realms of intensified dreaming—involving animals, gods, and death—in which the dynamism of spirit emerges with special vividness.

Part II

Realms

CHAPTER 4

Dreaming Earth
Animals and Nature

Lakota healer Good Lifeways Woman (her sacred name) dreamed
a big dream in 1975. She had fasted for a day and slept outside
on Bear Butte in present-day South Dakota, waiting in hopes of
a revelation.

> I was facing north, and fell asleep. In that state I saw a
> large shape approaching me. I assumed it was an eagle.
> It was so big that it almost covered the sky. When it got
> closer I could see that it was an owl. It looked at me with
> those same yellow eyes. Soon that owl took on the shape
> of a man. . . . The man drew a circle in the dirt. In the dirt
> appeared an owl's face and an eagle's face. A blue light
> was also present. It marched up my pipe stem. The blue
> light asked, "Are you ready? When you are ready, I will
> help you," and that blue light traveled all around me.

Good Lifeways Woman had wanted to better understand
the spontaneous visions she had experienced during a recent

ceremony, as she told historian of religions Lee Irwin, and that was the reason she had gone out to Bear Butte. She said it had taken her many years to learn the proper use of her dream powers and the most effective ways of applying them to healing. This particular dream at Bear Butte created a new connection between her and the spirits of the eagle and the owl, who became her personal guides and provided additional teachings in later dreams.

This story illustrates the powerful ritual practice of *dream incubation*, which involves sleeping in a special place in hopes of having a dream that responds to an important question or concern. Since the beginning of recorded history, people in cultures all over the world have performed dream incubation rites in one form or another. We have already seen one example of this, with the Yansi elders sleeping outside in quest of dreams that will help them determine the best timing for an important ceremony. In ancient China, India, Egypt, and Greece, dream incubation provided a resource for making decisions at all levels of society. The Australian Aboriginal practice of making journeys into the "Dreamtime" often involve a collective practice of dream incubation. Since medieval times, Muslims have privately performed the ritual of *istikhara*, in which they recite special prayers before sleep at a shrine or other holy place, seeking divine guidance about a particular question in waking life. Perhaps the earliest evidence of dream incubation appears in the beautifully surreal images painted by paleolithic humans in deep caves in present-day Spain and France, where they very likely performed group rituals, slept, and dreamed.

In most of these instances, the power of a dream incubation ritual seems to be amplified and perhaps even triggered by the natural setting in which the person sleeps. In other words, nature itself has a profoundly inspiring effect on our dreams. Mountains, forests, caves, beaches, deserts: if you lie down and go to sleep in these places, you are more likely to have a vivid, revelatory dream. Humans have known this for millennia and have derived many benefits from the nature-dreaming connection. In modern times, however, our relationship with the natural world has taken a drastic turn for the worse, to the point where environmental catastrophes loom on all sides and the climate is changing in violent, unpredictable ways. One of the oldest themes of spiritual dreaming—nature—has now become one of the most urgent sources of collective crisis.

In this chapter, we will look at how our interactions with the natural world impact our dreams and how dreams affect our environmental behaviors and attitudes. This dynamic appears most clearly with the dreams of animals, and that will be our focus. But it's important to note that nature-related themes can appear in dreams in other forms too: in vivid dreams of natural elements like water and fire, for instance, and in nightmares of dramatic natural disasters like storms, earthquakes, and tornadoes. All of these nature-related dreams can have metaphorical meanings *and* literal external-world references. We can recognize both metaphorical and literal meanings and, ideally, integrate them into a higher level of environmental awareness. By delving deeply into the inner wilderness of the dreaming imagination, we renew and revitalize our spiritual connection with the outer wilderness of the natural world.

The Study of Dream Content

In this chapter and the ones to come, I will refer to scientific studies on the patterns of content in various people's dreams.

Let's pause for a moment to look at how this kind of research—content analysis—informs a spiritually oriented approach to dreaming. At first glance, these studies might seem irrelevant to a spirituality of dreaming and perhaps even antagonistic to it. There are many reasons to be skeptical: the focus on numbers and statistics leads our attention far away from the lived reality of dreaming, the results have no apparent bearing on the practices of sharing or interpreting dreams, and the findings of these studies are taken more seriously by those in the academy than insights coming from experiential sources, thus potentially overshadowing valuable perspectives.

For many years, I was a harsh skeptic toward the use of quantitative methods to the study of dream content, such as the system of content analysis developed by Calvin Hall and Robert Van de Castle in 1966 and later updated by G. William Domhoff and Adam Schneider in 2008. Over time, however, I learned how to use this system in ways that can enhance the exploration of spirituality in dreaming. It took a great deal of effort, patience, and trial-and-error experimentation to reach this point, and I am grateful to Domhoff and Schneider for their help on several research studies in which we applied the Hall and Van de Castle (HVDC) system in new and unusual directions. By now, I feel confident that statistical methods like this one can play a valuable role in nearly any mode of studying dreams.

No special scientific training or mathematical skill is required here. The most useful features of the HVDC approach to content analysis are really just extensions of what your own mind could do if it could hold thousands of dreams in awareness at once. The HVDC system is an efficient way of sifting through huge numbers of dreams to count all the instances of various types of content—characters, emotions, settings, and social interactions, among others. The results of these tabulations provide a fascinating and highly informative self-portrait of your basic patterns of dreaming. The patterns may be obvious, or they may be shocking; but if the analysis is done properly, they will assuredly represent the actual empirical reality of what you do and don't dream about.

Once you become familiar with your dreams from this kind of statistical perspective, you can do a couple of fun and informative things. First, you can look for correlations between the patterns in your dreams and your activities, interests, and beliefs in waking life. Hall and Domhoff have termed this *the continuity hypothesis*, which suggests the more often an item appears in a dream, the more likely it has emotional significance in waking life. For example, if you dream frequently about dogs but never about cats, it's likely that dogs are emotionally important to you in the waking world and cats aren't. Dreams are filled with meaningful continuities like this, which statistical methods of analysis can help to identify and illuminate.

Second, you can look for areas where the patterns in your dreams do *not* reflect your waking-life activities. Following what I call *the discontinuity hypothesis*—deviations from the usual waking-dreaming continuities that can signal the arrival of new creative energies in the dreamer's awareness—some aspect of the psyche may emerge first in dreams before it can manifest fully in the waking world. Big dreams are often characterized by numerous discontinuities of this kind. This can give big dreams an appearance of nonsensical bizarreness, but they actually reflect the most creative, boundary-transcending powers of the imagination. If you look carefully at the weirdest, most unusual, and most anomalous contents of your dreams, you will very likely discover new dimensions of spiritual dynamism in your life.

In the late 1990s, Domhoff and Schneider developed a website, the Dreambank, devoted to dream research in the tradition of Hall and Van de Castle's content analysis system. After several years of experimenting with the Dreambank and consulting with Domhoff and Schneider, I created an online archive of research information, the SDDb, in 2009. This database now includes more than forty thousand dream reports from a wide variety of people, plus responses from dozens of demographic surveys asking people about their sleep and dream patterns. Most of the specific findings I cite in the coming pages are drawn from the SDDb, which means you can go directly to the site and look at the data for yourself. Maybe you'll see something I missed. In chapter 9, we will discuss how emerging technologies of data analysis are quickly transforming the study of dreams and bringing into view a host of new possible applications—some exciting and others frightening.

Fauna of the Dream World

"The dream world is well-populated," observed Mary Whiton Calkins, one of the unsung heroes of modern dream research. Writing in her 1893 article "Statistics of Dreams" in the *American Journal of Psychology*, Calkins examined two lengthy series of dreams, her own and those gathered from a colleague. She found, among other things, that nearly all the dreams included at least one other character besides the dreamer. Current research in content analysis supports her finding, suggesting that something like 95 percent of dreams have one or more characters. Most of these characters are humans, but many of them are animals. Let's look at some of the variations in which animals appear in dreams, how often, and to whom.

The SDDb includes a set of what I call *baselines*: dreams gathered from demographically diverse people who participated in a systematic research project. The baselines are not a perfectly representative picture of human dreaming, but they do give a broad-based picture of common patterns in the contents of people's dreams, at least for people living in present-day Western societies. In terms of dreams about animals, the baseline frequencies for women are 13 percent and for men 12 percent; this means 13 percent of the women's dreams in the baselines (about one in eight) included at least one reference to an animal, and 12 percent of the men's dreams had at least one animal reference. Men and women differ on various other categories of dream content—women have more fear and more family characters; men have more physical aggression and more transportation references. But with regard to animals in dreams, their overall frequencies are essentially the same. For both men and women, the most frequently mentioned animal is the dog, and they both dream frequently of fish and snakes. Women, however, dream much more often about cats than men do, while men tend to dream more of birds.

Two additional and highly significant findings from content analysis shed more light on dreams about animals. First, people in traditional, rural, non-Western communities tend to have more animals in their dreams than do people from modern urban Western societies. With the help of anthropologist D. Schneider, Hall compared dreams from several traditional rural groups with dreams from modern urban societies, and he found "the animal percent . . . is always higher for small-scale societies than it is for large-scale ones." In Domhoff's book *Finding Meaning in Dreams*, where he reports on Hall's study, he offers a plausible explanation: "Because these small-scale societies are in greater proximity to animals and nature than the urbanized populations from large-scale societies for whom we have dream reports, we think this difference in animal percent is a cultural difference revealing a relationship between dreams and waking life."

The second key finding here is that children tend to have more animals in their dreams than adults do. According to Domhoff, "The biggest difference between child and adult dreams on the character scales is the much larger number of animals in children's dream reports, which manifests itself as a higher animal percent." Explanations here include the influence of playing with stuffed animals, seeing animals in cartoons, and interacting with family pets, all of which are presumably more common among children than adults. Furthermore, for both children and adults from small-scale societies, dreams of animals often include aggression and violence, usually a direct attack on the dreamer. Animals carry great power in dreams, a power that is not always friendly to human interests and concerns.

As you may have anticipated, the appearance of animals in dreams can lead to wonderful discoveries of metaphorical insight, where the animal enables greater understanding of a previously unknown reality. For example, a vague sense of unease and frustration may be clarified by a vivid dream of a lion trapped in a cage, pacing back and forth. Inarticulate anger can manifest in a dream of a growling bear. Secret longing and attraction might prompt a dream of a fox on the prowl. As a general metaphor, animals in dreams often reflect the energies of the unconscious. To our conscious minds, our unconscious may have a vitality and nonhuman intelligence that seem almost animal-like.

These ideas become easier to understand when illustrated by actual dreams, so now we'll consider two examples. Looking at how humans relate to the animals in our dreams—how we treat them and how they treat us—can shed light on how we relate in waking life to our emotions, our desires, or what we sometimes call our *animal instincts*.

Of Whales and Bugs

Bei Linda Tang owns an organic textiles company in Vancouver, British Columbia, known as Dream Designs. Born in Wuhan, China, Linda came to the United States as a teenager, where she finished high school and then college in New York City. After working in the financial world of New York for several years, she moved to Vancouver to pursue entrepreneurial opportunities in products using organic cotton. She married her long-time boyfriend, purchased the Dream Designs company from its founder, and devoted the next several years to building the business. The work was long and arduous, taking a toll on her health and straining her relationship with her now husband. Fortunately, she attended a workshop on Zen meditation, and the practice gave her a new sense of peace and openness. She and her husband decided to have a child, and Linda felt that "pregnancy was easy and joyful; however, birth was stressful and trying." An avalanche of family drama immediately followed her daughter's arrival into the world, however, leaving Linda feeling sad and exhausted.

One night, a few months after the birth, she went to sleep and had a dream:

> In this dream I was hanging onto a zip line with hands and feet trying to move slowly and carefully across a storming ocean. The zip line is endless and suspended

20 meters above the waves. Two whales, a mother and a calf, emerged from the depth of the sea and blew water as they swam past underneath me, filling me with exhilaration, awe, and joy. The sheer joy I felt upon waking intrigued me because of the treacherous situation I was in. It also felt incredibly real. To this day when I think about it, I could still feel the sensation of cold vapor hitting my skin as the whales breathed out water from below me.

Initially, Linda did not know what to make of this dream. It was vivid and unforgettable, yet its meanings were elusive. Only ten years later did she really focus on the dream, study its contents, and try to develop an interpretation. This process ultimately prompted her to write a book called *Navigate Life with Dreams*. She said the dream might seem like a nightmare, with the perilous position above the ocean and the imminent danger of falling, but it actually felt extremely positive, "a high-spirited happy dream."

Using the metaphorical approach discussed earlier, we can see how each of the elements in the dream expresses a distinctive meaning, all of which come together to form what Linda called a "storyline." She associated the zip line over the stormy ocean with the long, frightening, uncertain transition in her life brought on by the birth of her daughter. How does she feel as a new mother with a strained marriage and a demanding business? Like she's hanging on to a thin wire high above a deep, swirling ocean.

But from this position, she is able to see an amazing sight: two whales swimming through the water. For Linda, the whales represented her sense of spirituality, her connection with the greater powers of the universe, and the deep joy and peace she found in meditation. Whales are an active and familiar presence in the waters off the Vancouver coast, and for many people, their enormous size and graceful intelligence naturally elicit spiritual feelings of wonder and awe. In Linda's dream, it's not just any two whales but a mother and her calf, which she regarded as a direct reference to her maternal instincts emerging from the unconscious, metaphorically expressed by the ocean. The spray of water vapor from their spouts, a primal blast of dream *pneuma*, creates a direct connection between her and the whales, filling her with a positive new energy that carried over into her waking life. At a very difficult time in Linda's life, one of the most powerful animals on earth comes in a dream to *inspire* her with a deeply compelling image of unconscious wisdom and family devotion.

The second example involves dream animals at the opposite end of the zoological scale. In the summer of 1991, Michael R. Dupré attended an international conference titled "Dreaming in Russia," organized by Jungian analyst Robert Bosnak. Held at a conference center just outside Moscow, the meeting brought together dream researchers from North America, Europe, and various parts of what was then the Soviet Union. I was one of the attendees, too, and Michael and I were assigned to share a room. I had met Michael briefly at an earlier dream studies conference in the United States, and I knew he was struggling with his health due to AIDS. This was early in the epidemic, when no effective treatments were yet available and misconceptions about AIDS abounded. When we first reached the dormitory at the Russian conference center, he asked if I was okay with him being my roommate. I said yes, of course, and apologized that he even needed to ask.

Yet while I had zero problems with Michael, I was still freaking out. We had apparently arrived in Russia on the very day that the Soviet Red Army launched a coup against Mikhail Gorbachev: August 19, 1991. As our group's bus drove away from the airport that day, a stream of massive tanks and armored personnel carriers drove toward it; ours was one of the last foreign flights that landed before the Moscow airport was shut down. I have written elsewhere about my experiences at the conference; here, I will simply relate what Michael said in an article titled "Russia. Dreaming. Liberation," which he wrote for the journal *Dreaming*.

The surreal transformation of a dreams conference into a geopolitical nightmare actually seemed to make sense to Michael in ways the rest of us struggled to comprehend. "Having AIDS certainly has put me into contact with my own mortality," he wrote. "Of course, living with this knowledge is at the very least a two-edged sword. People with AIDS are constantly living 'under the sword,' knowing it could drop at any moment. Another edge is the realization of the importance of doing and living what brings out the passion in your soul. That is what brought me to this conference on dreams. I've cultivated my dreams like a garden, ever so slowly, since about the age of four."

During the conference, we all tried to keep up with the violent, fast-paced events happening just a few miles away. The army was occupying Red Square, and crowds of protestors were rushing to the city center. Mikhail Gorbachev had gone into hiding, while the mayor of Moscow, Boris Yeltsin, was barricaded in his official residence, defying the army's attempt to take control of the city. Who was in charge of the coup? With Gorbachev gone, who was in charge of the country? Where was this whole situation going anyway? No one could say. All communications with the outside world were cut off, and any thoughts we might have had about trying to leave the country were out of the question. So having no other options, we simply went ahead with the conference.

The meeting included several forms of group dream-sharing. Michael had the opportunity to share the following dream, which he had while at the conference, with people from an unusually wide variety of national backgrounds. "I dream that I'm in my room at the conference center," he told us. "Suddenly, I notice there are a number of bugs, of different shapes and sizes, on the walls. The scariest ones are these two big knob-shaped black bugs. I think I cannot live with them, and I go to get a shoe to smash them. I also think how disgusting that's going to be. I turn around, and they've crawled down the wall behind the storage space, making it very difficult if not impossible to be rid of them." The animal at the center of his dream attracted keen attention and interest—"It seemed that everyone related to bugs," he wrote later. Unlike the massive, beautiful, smoothly swimming whales of Linda's dream, the bugs in Michael's dream are small, disgusting creatures crawling into the corners and shadows of his room. The metaphorical possibilities with bugs are numerous: to bug someone is to annoy them; an illness is a bug; to bug out is to leave fast; a bug is a listening device; bugs are a lower form of life, yet they are far more numerous than we are, a constant threat of plague, infestation, and illness; bugs are also essential creatures in the vast network of terrestrial life, without whom we could not survive. The group's discussion of Michael's dream ranged widely, filling him with new insights. "The main metaphor for me was the 'I spy bug,'" Michael wrote. "Somebody's watching, somebody's listening, somebody unknown. The collective anxiety and fear and paranoia had entered my psyche as if by osmosis. I was not immune. Not immune."

Michael had other vivid, important dreams during the week of the conference, but this one beautifully illustrates the special impact of animals in dreams, with metaphorical meanings that resonate across differences of culture and nationality. Sadly, Michael died a couple of years after the conference. The gathering clearly affected him deeply and gave him precious gifts for his journey onward.

I never did ask him an admittedly personal question about this particular dream—which, after all, was set in the room at the conference center where I was sleeping too. Did he feel *I* was a bug? Was his roommate—me—the "somebody unknown," watching and listening to him in his private space? These questions echoed bigger anxieties about surveillance and discrimination against gay men like Michael during an era of widespread homophobia. Even though I was consciously fine being his roommate, had I unknowingly behaved in ways that made him uncomfortable? I can't be sure I didn't, and that haunts me.

The Spirit of Plants

The living beings of the plant world also make their presence known in dreaming. Our familiarity with various kinds of plants enables them to represent metaphorical meanings at all three levels we discussed in chapter 2: the personal, the cultural, and the universal. Plants and trees can carry personal meaning (redwood trees signify childhood for people who grew up near redwoods), cultural (love is a red rose; temptation is an apple), and universal (fertility is a fruit; hidden strength is a root). Some big dreams contain vibrant settings with an abundance of plants—forests, jungles, gardens, meadows—that reflect the dynamic growth potential within the unconscious itself.

Turning from the metaphorical to the literal, some plants can be used as dream-stimulating agents. Incubation rituals often involve eating, drinking, or smoking plant-based substances intended to elicit especially powerful dreams. The healers and shamans of traditional cultures look to their dreams for insights into the nature and uses of the various flora in their local environment. Sometimes a dream of plants can lead to transformative actions in honor of plants in the waking world. Several years ago, I met a US Forest Service professional named Herbert Schroeder, who researched different ways Americans value our national parks. Conventional approaches to forest management emphasized timber harvesting and fire suppression, with *recreation* as a catch-all phrase for all the other ways people interact with nature. Schroeder was trying to develop a more sophisticated and nuanced understanding of these recreational values, which he believed should also include the aesthetic enjoyment and spiritual revitalization that many people experience in natural settings. *Recreation* was too simple and narrow a category, he thought, to contain all the value people find in the natural world apart from its "uses."

Schroeder and I discussed dreams as a possible source of insight into these specific kinds of nature-related values, and I persuaded him to attend a dream research conference to share his work as part of a panel on dreams and the environment. In his presentation, he told the story of a colleague's dream, one that played a pivotal role in that colleague's choice of a new career:

A number of years ago, when I was working/living in a field unrelated to the environment, forests, natural resources, etc., I had a dream. This dream opened a new door—leading me to new work and thought, to an area that fits my life in a way no other way has. . . . This is what I remember of it: I was facing east, deep in a forest of large, old trees. The foliage was dense, perhaps there were vines or moss in the trees, adding to the depth and shades of green. Sunlight was making its way through the green—from the east (maybe an hour after sunrise). Mostly the sun made the leaves glow, some shafts pierced through. There was a communication between the trees and I—not verbal yet not ephemeral either. There was a rightness, a sureness I felt in being there, as well as an excitement, a charge. I woke with a line in my head: "That's what I do with my life—it's with the big green stuff." (The "big green stuff" is trees.) Since that time I have pursued an advanced degree, changed jobs and have "come down where I ought to be" (in the words of the Shaker hymn).

Schroeder said the person would only share the dream with him and give him permission to retell it on the condition that it be kept completely anonymous, with no other personally identifying details included in the report. "The reason for this condition was a fear that admitting to being so influenced by a dream would lead to a loss of credibility as a natural resource professional," Schroeder writes.

When Schroeder first told me this story, I was both pleased and distressed. Pleased because a dream had played a helpful role in mediating someone's discovery of their passion and calling in life. Distressed because the person felt compelled to hide this beautiful truth about themselves for fear of being judged by others. Who knows how many other people have experienced similar dreams that could have led to a positive change in their waking lives?

We know that flora and fauna inhabit human dreams. Now let's look at the relationship from the other direction and consider what *they* may be dreaming about *us*.

Do Animals Dream?

For millennia, humans have recognized that when animals sleep, they display virtually all the behaviors we associate with dreaming. Anyone who has dogs or cats as pets knows that animals show all the signs of dreaming while they are asleep. Their whiskers twitch, their paws tense and jerk, their breathing increases, they make strange growls and whimpers, and if you look closely enough, you can see their eyes moving beneath their closed lids. When we see a person who is asleep and behaving in these ways, we can assume they are in the midst of a dream. So it's easy to infer our pet dogs and cats are dreaming too.

The difference, of course, is that when the person wakes up, we can ask them if they were dreaming, and if so, what they were dreaming about. Lacking a direct means of communication, we cannot do that with animals. Their inner worlds remain closed to us. Because of this apparent barrier between humans and animals, the question of whether animals dream has long appeared to have no chance of an objective scientific answer. We can infer that animals dream, we can observe countless details that make it look like they're dreaming, but we cannot truly *know* that they dream.

In the absence of sure knowledge, many contemporary researchers have taken what may seem the wisest course: assuming that animals do *not* dream. Two unfortunate cultural biases join forces here: a bias against dreaming and a bias against the idea that animals possess inner mental states of any kind, waking or dreaming. Only in recent years has enough research accumulated to push back on a stubborn scientific bias that focuses strictly on external behavior and denies that animals have an inner mental life with thoughts, emotions, and genuine dreams. So the short answer is: yes, animals dream. The real question is: Why has it taken us so long to figure that out?

One way to measure the strength of these negative attitudes toward the idea of the dream life of animals is to consider the results of experiments conducted in the 1950s and 1960s by Michel Jouvet, a French neuroscientist and sleep expert who coined the term *paradoxical sleep*. Jouvet's research focused on the sleep and potential dream behaviors of cats, and he designed a study that, while cruel to the felines (as nearly all such studies are), yielded highly significant findings. Jouvet started with the known fact that during paradoxical sleep, the brain is highly aroused, but the body remains essentially motionless. A particular mechanism in the brainstem acts as a gatekeeper during sleep, blocking the signals from the brain so they do not trigger the corresponding physical actions in the body. What would happen, Jouvet wondered, if that gatekeeper were removed so the signals from the sleeping brain could go straight to the rest of the body?

He performed the necessary surgical procedure on a group of cats and then observed them while they slept. Sure enough, instead of remaining motionless, the cats enacted a variety of primal, survival-related behaviors. They hissed with their ears back as if in a fight, ran around their enclosure in apparent chase of prey, sniffed and explored the space with curiosity, and mounted stationary objects in evident sexual arousal—all while fully asleep. If such behaviors do indeed represent cats "acting out" their dreams, the contents of those dreams certainly sound familiar from decades of research on human dreams.

Despite Jouvet's dramatic findings, for the next several decades, the mainstream of Western science remained resolutely agnostic about whether animals have dreams, thoughts, feelings, or any other forms of what humans experience as consciousness. After all, the skeptics would say, look how easily we project human qualities into inanimate objects; scientists must be careful to avoid anthropomorphism in their explanations of nature. Any evidence in favor of animal mental states can always be explained as the byproduct of something else, a mechanical reflex without any intention or purpose behind it. According to the premise of Occam's razor—that a simpler explanation should be favored over an unnecessarily complex one—animal behaviors could always be explained most simply as purely physiological reflexes with no mental content required.

At a certain point, we can fairly wonder if the debate about the dream lives of animals is no longer about evidence but about philosophy. This is the thesis of David M. Peña-Guzmán's excellent book *When Animals Dream: The Hidden World of Animal Consciousness*. As he traces the history of modern Western research and theorizing about animal dreams, Peña-Guzmán makes the remarkable—and disheartening—discovery that an earlier scientific tradition, culminating in the 1800s, recognized that many animals have rich and complex mental lives, including a capacity for dreaming. But with the behaviorist revolution in twentieth-century psychology, the premise took hold that only external actions could be observed, measured, and analyzed in truly scientific terms. Anything having to do with the inner thoughts, feelings, or images of an organism was excluded from serious consideration.

Now the time has come, Peña-Guzmán argues, to flip the historical script. "Our collective error was not that we considered humans and the other animals on a continuum of mental activities during the nineteenth century, but rather that we turned our backs on this continuist perspective in the twentieth and, as a result, our perception of animals changed for the worse," he writes. "We began seeing their lives as so deficient, so dull, so bare, and so contemptible in comparison to ours that, in an act of collective self-delusion, we convinced ourselves that they could not possibly have what we have: a meaningful inner world. *That* was our mistake."

Peña-Guzmán cites dozens of recent studies providing evidence that various animals have sleep experiences that merit the term *dreaming*. Here are a few brief examples of the most striking of these studies.

* A sleeping octopus was observed engaging in all the actions involved in catching and eating a crab, including the dramatic and precise changes in skin color (from white to yellow-orange, then vivid purple, then a light gray-green) that would normally accompany a successful hunt in waking.

* When rats, after being trained in a complex maze, went to sleep, the part of the brain known as the hippocampus, which processes new physical skills, became active and played out the exact same neurological patterns, in the same amount of time, as when the rats were awake and actually moving through the maze. This is what we would expect to see if the rats were dreaming about the task they had just been trained to perform in waking.

* The complex mating songs that one generation of zebra finches teaches to the next generation require a great

deal of neurological activity to learn and perform. Researchers have observed, during zebra finch sleep, that these same brain patterns are associated with learning the songs. Not only do the "dream songs" last as long as the ones in waking but the zebra finch's vocal cords expand and contract in sleep just as they do when singing in the waking state. Peña-Guzmán notes the important quality of *embodiment* here—something that many researchers believe is a crucial quality of human dreaming too.

✳ Chimpanzees trained to communicate in American Sign Language have been observed during sleep making hand gestures that, were they made in waking, would be recognized by the researchers as authentic signs. Among the words they signed during sleep were *coffee*, *good*, and *more*. In waking, signs are always directed toward someone else; during sleep, though, the chimpanzees made the signs in the absence of anyone in their external environment. Their sleep behavior was consistent with the internal experience of communicating with a character in a dream.

✳ An experiment with rhesus monkeys trained them to press a bar when seeing an image or else receive an electric shock. When the monkeys slept and entered REM, they would suddenly press the bar vigorously, just as they did in waking. According to the researchers, "Sometimes they also made facial grimaces, flared nostrils, breathed deeply, and even barked as they pressed the bar. Presumably they were 'seeing things' during these intervals of rapid eye movements and were avoiding the shock associated with the images."

✳ Several studies have indicated that animals can suffer nightmares, such as those prompted by experiments that, if humans were the subjects, would be considered a form of torture. Especially disturbed sleep has been observed among elephants and apes who, earlier in life, witnessed the killing of family members and are still traumatized by the experience.

These studies do more than demonstrate the fact that animals dream. They also begin to show the contours of what animals dream *about*. A zoological baseline of dream content will likely include these high-frequency themes: eating, hunting, grooming, having sex, play-fighting—and nightmares about humans. The evidence already supports a version of the continuity hypothesis in animal dreaming insofar as animals seem to dream frequently about important, survival-related concerns in their waking lives.

More than one hundred years ago, Freud noted exactly this point. "I do not myself know what animals dream of," he wrote. "But a proverb, to which my attention was drawn by one of my students, does claim to know. 'What,' asks the proverb, 'do geese dream of?' And it replies: 'Of maize [corn].' The whole theory that dreams are wish-fulfillments is contained in these two phrases."

This may be true. Yet we should be careful not to let our human assumptions about dreaming prematurely limit what we can learn about animal dreaming. So far, we are only seeing reflections of our dream patterns in the dreams of other creatures. But what might they be dreaming that we cannot easily recognize? Do animals have their own prototypical dreams? Do they ever dream of being a different kind of animal? Does a cat dream of being a bird? Do they ever dream of being human, as we periodically dream of being another animal? Might the dreams of all terrestrial species emerge from a collective unconscious rooted in our shared planetary existence?

These are questions for the not-too-distant future as we finally get past the long overdue recognition that many animals do genuinely dream. It may be hard to imagine right now, but one day we may move forward together to develop mutually respectful practices of interspecies dream-sharing and interpretation.

Dreamers of the Earth

My first book, *The Wilderness of Dreams*, used an extended metaphor of dreaming as a kind of wilderness. The various disciplines of dream research—psychology, neuroscience, anthropology, art, and other fields—represent different paths that all lead into those wild, unknown lands. As a way of characterizing the power and impact of highly memorable big dreams, I offered the concept of *root metaphors*: a special kind of metaphor that reaches into the most fertile depths of the psyche and becomes a perennially living source of meaning, orientation, and guidance in life. The "big green stuff" in Herbert Schroeder's friend's dream certainly qualifies as a root metaphor in this sense, as do Linda's two whales. Now that we know nonhuman creatures also have the capacity to dream, isn't it likely they have the capacity for big dreams, too, enabling them to use what they know to understand better what they don't know?

Let's consider one more finding about animal dreams cited by Peña-Guzmán. Researchers have found evidence of paradoxical sleep and dreamlike behaviors among cephalopods, including cuttlefish and octopuses. These creatures differ drastically, in evolutionary terms, from humans, primates, and all other mammals.

It's one thing to imagine your cat's dreams; it may feel like another thing entirely to imagine a fish's. "The discovery of oneiric behaviors in this group is particularly startling, for it implies that dreaming may have evolved independently in at least two phyla (*Chordata* and *Mollusca*)," writes Peña-Guzmán. "If true, this would have colossal implications for contemporary dream research." Vast genetic distances separate these species from our own, yet we now know the waking-sleeping-dreaming cycle has arisen independently multiple times through evolutionary history. This is strong evidence with truly "colossal implications" that this innate cycle of highly structured neural activation has profound value for many forms of life.

To explore dreaming, then, is to explore a realm of our lives that truly connects us not only to other people but to other forms of animal life on earth. We humans are, by nature, dreamers. Yet nature has not limited the oneiric capacity to the human species alone. The emerging truth is that we—humans and animals alike—dream our way through life. How might we be changed by the realization that we live on a *planet* of dreamers?

CHAPTER 5

Cosmic Conduit
Gods and Demons

For millennia, people in cultures all over the world have paid attention to the religious dimensions of their dreams. This does not mean they viewed all their dreams as religiously significant. They recognized that a large portion of dreams refer to the daily concerns of ordinary life without any further religious relevance. But they also recognized that some dreams have striking qualities—intense emotions, vibrant imagery, dramatic interactions, and existential themes—that stimulate religious ideas and spiritual feelings upon awakening.

Dreaming is a kind of primal wellspring of religious experience, influencing not only people's beliefs about God and the gods but also their conceptions of the soul, the afterlife, heaven, hell, demons, and a host of other theological beliefs. Historians and anthropologists have now found increasing evidence to support this very old idea. And we can likely intuit why this would be the case: that is, the psychospiritual intensity of dreaming can transform an abstract idea into a deeply relevant and personally meaningful conviction.

Whenever someone has a dream with vivid religious imagery, several questions often come to their minds upon awakening. Why *me*? Why did I have this dream with these incredible contents? Is there something wrong with me? Am I being tempted, or singled out, or chosen for something? How does this dream relate to my religious beliefs? To the religious beliefs of my community? What should I do with this special dream and its potent energies?

Such questions go to the heart of an individual's existential view of the world. The process of exploring these remarkable dreams thus becomes a kind of personalized journey of theological self-discovery. This is what I take philosopher Paul Ricoeur to be suggesting when he writes in his 1967 book *The Symbolism of Evil*, "It is in dreams that one can catch sight of the most fundamental and stable symbolisms of humanity passing from the 'cosmic' function to the 'psychic' function." In other words, dreaming represents a conduit for energy that moves between the cosmic and the psychic dimensions of life. In Ricoeur's philosophy, this mediating role of dreams has enormous significance because, as one of the most famous phrases from this book suggests, "the symbol gives rise to thought." Ricoeur proposes that our higher functions of reasoning are grounded in and animated by the autonomous activities of the symbolizing imagination. These activities reach into the unconscious realms of the psyche, the territory of Freud and Jung and other depth psychologists. But for Ricoeur, these symbolic products of dreaming lead *beyond* the personal sphere to connect us with the cosmic sphere of divine potentiality. Into the realm of gods and demons.

We turn now to the vital role of dreams in people's religious beliefs and practices. We will look at the special challenges of trying to interpret religiously charged dreams, and we will consider a helpful system for mapping the varieties of these kinds of dreams, especially ones with transcendent qualities like those found in dreams about God, gods, and other divine beings. We will also look at dreams of demons, devils, monsters, and other evil spirits. Jung's notion of the shadow archetype can help us understand the paradoxical value of nightmares with these kinds of frightening characters. Beyond the benefits for personal growth, an exploration of shadow imagery in dreams also contributes to a greater awareness of the unconscious roots of social prejudices and collective biases.

The Risk of Getting It Wrong

If we grant that dreams can provide an authentic connection with the powers of the divine (however one conceives such powers), then the challenge becomes figuring out how to interpret these kinds of dreams. How can we determine whether a given dream really does convey a spiritually valuable insight or if it merely reflects an ordinary concern from personal life? Or worse: What if it might be a seductive false dream sent by a malicious supernatural being to mislead us? How are you supposed to know which of these categories applies to your dream? The stakes are very high.

The anxiety about making a mistake in either direction—assuming a nonreligious dream is *religious* (we could call it a false positive) or assuming a religiously meaningful dream is *insignificant* (a false negative)—has led to various efforts throughout history to categorize dreams, clarify their distinctions, and streamline their interpretations. Many religious traditions have developed a three-part system, along the lines of what I have just suggested: (1) dreams from the divine, (2) dreams from ordinary life, and (3) dreams from demonic forces.

For example, an influential typology of dreams in Islamic culture first appeared in the *Muqaddimah* (*An Introduction to History*) by the fourteenth-century scholar Ibn Khaldun. In his view, which extended Aristotle's philosophy of dreaming into a Muslim theological context, sleep is a time when our attention withdraws from the external world, liberating the mind to explore itself and the cosmos without limit or boundary. He wrote:

> Real dream vision is an awareness on the part of the rational soul in its spiritual essence, of glimpses of the forms of events. . . . God created man in such a way that the veil of the senses could be lifted through sleep, which is a natural function of man. When that veil is lifted, the soul is ready to learn the things it desires to know in the world of Truth. At times, it catches a glimpse of what it seeks. . . . Clear dream visions are from God. Allegorical dream visions, which call for interpretation, are from the angels. And "confused dreams" are from Satan, because they are altogether futile, as Satan is the source of futility.

Many Indigenous communities around the world make similar distinctions in their dreams. For instance, the Mohave people of the US Southwest speak of the traditional power-bestowing dream, *sumach ahot*, "dream lucky," versus the less significant, everyday dream. The Mehinaku people of central Brazil pay special attention to *jepuni yaja*, or "true dreams," which can herald life-changing insights. Ordinary, everyday dreams, *jepuni he te* ("mere dreams") do have some potential meaning but more likely in relation to everyday affairs and concerns and nothing beyond that. The first Hawaiians classified most dreams as *me ka noonoo mua ole*, or "unpremeditated": that is, unrelated to a religious ceremonial purpose, insignificant, and probably untrue. They considered a rare few dreams to be "premeditated," *i loaa mamuli o ka mana'o*: related to a religious purpose, highly significant, and likely to be true.

Still, the practical question remains of how exactly to determine whether a dream should be assigned to one category or another. The hyperrealism of dreaming and its seemingly infinite creativity enable any and every kind of content to appear. There appears no obvious way to draw clear lines between dreams that are true and false, or divine and demonic, or significant and insignificant. Perhaps such lines do not even exist. Consider the shocking episode at the beginning of Homer's *Iliad*, in which Zeus, the greatest of the ancient Greek gods, sends an intentionally misleading and harmful "evil dream" to the Greek general Agamemnon, urging him to launch his army into a battle the gods have already decreed he shall lose. How can we put faith in the meanings of any dreams when it's possible the gods themselves are using our dreams to deceive us?

In the long Islamic tradition of interpreting dreams, reaching back to the legendary dream scholar Ibn Sirin in the eighth century CE, a principle has emerged that a dream in which Muhammad appears must be true and reliable because Satan cannot take the form of the Prophet. For Muslims, this provides a kind of oneiric anchor—a reliable point of stability and clarity amid all the other uncertainties of dreaming. Christians have nothing comparable in their teachings about dreams, which has led in some instances to a rejection of all dreams as too complex and confusing. For instance, the sixteenth-century Protestant reformer Martin Luther prayed to God for *no* dreams, true or false, because he found it too difficult to distinguish between them with confidence. "I care nothing about visions and dreams," Luther wrote. "Although they seem to have meaning, yet I despise them and am content with the sure meaning and trustworthiness of Holy Scripture."

This comment from Luther highlights a larger tension between dreams and religious traditions. A religious tradition is a community's set of the most valuable ideas, beliefs, and practices from the past that structure people's present-day life. Dreams, however, can and often do range far *beyond* the bounds of the dreamer's religious tradition, leading into "taboo" territory of heretical experiences and religiously forbidden activities. And yet the unorthodox tendencies of dreaming also open the way to spiritual innovations, bursts of creativity, and novel solutions to collective problems. This poses a crucial challenge for every religious tradition. Block out dreams, and you block out a true source of religious vitality and growth. Let dreams in, and you let in a whirlwind of destabilizing, possibly revolutionary energies.

There is no single right way to balance these concerns; each tradition manages the tension in its own fashion. As a broad generalization, I would say dreams tend to be more central in religious groups that exist on the periphery of their larger societies, while dreams tend to be more peripheral in religious groups that exist at the center of their larger societies. In other words, if a religious tradition has a high degree of social power and status, it is less likely to view dreams as a positive, helpful resource and more likely to reject dreams as irrelevant or possibly dangerous.

If a religious tradition has low social authority and exists on the margins of the mainstream culture, it is more likely to welcome dreams and their transcendent visions of otherworldly realities.

Four Clusters of Dreams

Modern researchers have developed their own systems for classifying and categorizing dreams. Jung's distinction between big and little dreams is one of these models. My notion of four dream prototypes—aggressive, sexual, gravitational, and mystical—is another. Others have used terms like *highly memorable dreams*, *intensified dreams, apex dreams*, and *culture pattern dreams* to shed light on the same basic realm of oneiric phenomena. Here, I want to share a contemporary typology that has value for a spiritual approach to dreaming, even if that was not the model's original aim.

Canadian psychologist Don Kuiken, along with his colleagues Shelley Sikora, Ria Busink, and others, has looked closely at the reports that people give of "dreams that continued to influence their thoughts and feelings even after awakening." This approach has the benefit of emphasizing the actual consequences of the dream in the waking world, potentially giving us new insights into the dreams that have the most tangible effects on our lives outside of sleep. Despite its primarily psychological framework, the Kuiken approach helps to clarify a few different types of religiously significant dreams.

The first of Kuiken's four categories, or clusters, is *mundane dreams*. These dreams have few emotions, no vivid imagery, and no special significance. They lack vigorous activities and have few visual discontinuities (such as visual anomalies, shifts in setting, and explicit-looking behavior); everything is rather vague and fragmentary. They represent, in short, *non*-impactful dreams. The primary qualities of the other three categories Kuiken describes are absent from this one. An example of a mundane dream might involve you driving a car alone on an unknown city street past a strange building. Nothing much happens, you don't know where you are or where you're going, and it all seems hazy and indistinct. Dreams like this generally do not have a strong effect on waking life.

The dreams in the second cluster involve feelings of *agony and distress*, usually as a result of an experience of separation, loss, death, or disillusionment. These are painful and upsetting dreams with many negative qualities, and yet they also include enhanced sensibilities such as strongly positive feelings of meaning, knowledge, and awareness. A typical dream from this cluster would be a dream of a dead person returning and inter-acting with the dreamer; even if the interaction was positive, the individual often awakens feeling sad and mournful. (More discussion of such dreams will come in the next chapter.) In later writings, Kuiken and his colleagues termed these *existential dreams* because of the way they evoke thoughts and feelings about mortality, death, and the meaning of life.

The third cluster involves classic *nightmare* themes of intense fear and harm avoidance. These dreams have the strongest emotional energy of all the clusters. Most of the scenarios depicted actions of fighting and fleeing, with the dreamer doing most of the fleeing, trying to avoid physical injury and death. Kuiken found high levels of narrative coherence in these dreams, sometimes with long, continuous action sequences. A typical example would be a chasing dream in which an evil antagonist is attacking the dreamer, who runs and tries to hide but can never completely escape. The visual imagery can be extremely realistic and lifelike, eliciting a deep instinctual response from the dreamer. In these nightmares, people's self-awareness was lower than in the dreams from the other clusters; they noticed fewer anomalies and had little self-reflection during the dream. The intensity of the fear aroused in these dreams apparently consumes the sleeping mind, overwhelming other thoughts and emotions.

The existential dreams of cluster 2 and even some of the nightmares of cluster 3 can carry spiritual dimensions, but the dreams in Kuiken's research that demonstrate the most spiritual impact have a set of shared characteristics that he terms *transcendent*. These dreams in cluster 4 can be both surprising and revelatory. People feel these dreams have extraordinary meaning for them and yet cannot express this meaning in ordinary language. Some of the frequent themes in transcendent dreams include feelings of awe, tremendous energy, and brilliant aesthetic beauty. They tend to have a high degree of self-awareness, with multiple perspectives and levels of insight. A typical dream in cluster 4 might be an otherworldly journey, or an experience of magical healing, or an ecstatic encounter with a god. Whatever their contents, these dreams have the shared quality of making an immediate, tangible, and lasting impact on the individual upon awakening.

Setting aside the mundane dreams cluster, Kuiken says the other three types of impactful dreams can be characterized by hyperrealism, visual discontinuities, and incredibly strong emotions, sometimes stronger than anything we experience in waking.

Before we explore how these ideas play out in some actual examples, let's pause for a moment to marvel at the creative genius of the mind in sleep. The mind's capacity to generate incredibly vivid and deeply immersive life-worlds, with zero external input, is truly one of the wonders of human psychology.

Far from shutting down in sleep, our minds actually seem to find a whole new gear of creativity. The temporary detachment from the outside world when we sleep has the effect of releasing the imagination and opening our minds to a wider range of meaningful associations and connections.

Core of Being

Grace (not her real name) shared with her therapist several dreams she had about God. During the course of their therapeutic work together, Grace learned to recognize some of her dreams as important steps in her recovery from an emotionally abusive upbringing and now hopefully moving toward a reconnection with her spiritual yearnings and creative powers.

Grace's therapist, Bonnelle Lewis Strickling, was a Jungian therapist and spiritual director in British Columbia who also taught in the philosophy department at Simon Fraser University. Bonnelle was a good friend and colleague of mine, and even after her death, she continues to influence me and others who are drawn to the endlessly fertile intersection of psychology, philosophy, and spirituality. Bonnelle wrote about Grace and one of her dreams in her 2007 book *Dreaming about the Divine*, in which she relates several fascinating and thought-provoking dreams from her clients over the years.

Toward the end of therapy, as Grace was preparing to renew her social life, seek out healthy relationships, and perhaps have a family one day, she had this dream, which Bonnelle recounted in *Dreaming about the Divine*:

> I find myself in a large white room, an open space with a slanting roof, entirely composed of windows. It is an

attic open to the sunlight that dazzles the room. There with me is a great broad man with a wild head of white hair, a rumpled face, and soulful brown eyes, wearing a white lab coat. He reminds me of a giant Einstein, and I know it has to be God. The way he looks at me at his side as he busily moves around the room makes me know that I am working for God, that I'm his assistant. Of courses the real tip-off is that I'm also wearing a white lab coat. God shows me what he made and what we two are working on, creating new beings. Lying on a bed, the bed I had as a child, are three figures. They look like wax baby dolls at first. As I step close to what kind of wonders God is up to, I see the dolls are human and fleshy, and they aren't babies but baby-sized beings with adult bodies, both male and female. Their faces aren't worn, marred by time and hardship, but fresh and pure, like grown-ups who are magical babies again, and so are truly born again. They lie on the bed not breathing; but not dead, yet not alive. God tells me to get the "Animating Spirit." At least that is what I think he said. He said it in Latin, I suspect. I'm not sure, but I get the gist, and I certainly don't want to mess up, not on my first day on the job with God. I turn to God's cupboard, a lovely old oak Gothic dish cabinet that I inherited from my mother, something she loved. . . . Through the glass of the cupboard I see rows of sparks of light. Oh, no. They all look the same to me. Yet, I know that they are all the spirits and forces that God possesses, and they all look identical. But one. There is a warmer light, one that feels hot to me. "That must be the life force," I think. I take it out of the cupboard cupped in my hands, holding the light like a butterfly, one of fire but never burning. Right away I present the light to God. He looks at me sideways like I'm a bit of a goof. "That's not animating spirit," he says, "that's core of being." For a moment I know that the light I have is not what is going to bring these new beings to life. And as that knowledge reaches me, it wakes me.

A long dream like this, filled with complex details, can seem overwhelming at first. Where to start the analysis? We can try applying some of the methods and concepts we've learned to this dream to see if anything comes up.

In terms of Kuiken's "impactful dreams" theory, Grace's experience has many qualities of a transcendent dream, including supernatural powers, magical phenomena, and unusual perspectives. It made a very strong impression on Grace after she awoke: "I woke with a wonderful feeling of being aligned with God," she told Bonnelle. The dream portrays God in an unorthodox form, however: as a human scientist. If Grace had had this dream at another time in Christian history and shared it, she might have suffered harsh criticism—or worse—for such a heretical vision of the divine. The intensity of transcendent dreams can quickly lead into thickets of theological uncertainty. Whether this uncertainty becomes a cause for anxious repression or an opportunity for new spiritual growth depends on the dreamer's cultural context. Fortunately for Grace, she had Bonnelle as a therapist to help her learn how to create space in her waking life for her dream's unconventionally transcendent energies.

In Mageo's three-part model of metaphors in dreams, which we looked at in chapter 2, the references to Albert Einstein and the white lab coats can be seen as *cultural* metaphors, which would probably not make sense to people living outside of contemporary Western society. Within that society, Einstein is a recognizable figure with a reputation as one of the smartest people in history. A white lab coat is the cultural uniform of a modern scientist. These cultural details give more specificity to the overarching metaphor of being God's "assistant." How does Grace relate to God at this stage of her life as she finishes therapy with Bonnelle and embarks on a host of new activities? According to this dream, it's like she's an assistant in Einstein's science laboratory.

In addition to these cultural metaphors, Grace's dream also includes a *universal* metaphor around the care of new life, something familiar in its general features to everyone in all cultures. What exactly are she and God doing together? Bringing new life into being and nurturing it into maturity. Grace did have increasing thoughts about having children at some point in the future, so this universal metaphor had thought-provoking significance for her at a literal level in addition to its metaphorical reference to her writings, relationships, and other creative pursuits.

In terms of *personal* metaphors, Grace's dream included the reference to her childhood bed, the cupboard from her grandmother, and the number three, which she associated with her immediate family (mother, father, sister). These personal reference points bring the dream's meaning into the context of her painful family history, the fear and suffering she endured for years, and her newfound health and sense of groundedness in a living spiritual connection with God.

In many dreams, the action hinges on a moment of surprise—suddenly something new happens, something unexpected and disruptive to the situation. I have found such moments can provide valuable insights into the creative dynamics of the dream, highlighting a specific opportunity for change and transformation. In Grace's dream, the surprise comes in her misidentification of the light from the cupboard as "animating spirit." This is what she believes God asked her to retrieve. Initially confused by all the possibilities, she decides to follow her intuition and selects the light that seems warmest to her. And here is the surprise: God tells her she got it wrong. She has selected "core of being," not "animating spirit." Uh oh . . . now what? The light that Grace chose will *not* bring these three dolls to life. So what *will*? The dream leaves her with this open question—but still with the very positive feeling of being "aligned with God."

Grace told Bonnelle that she felt the dream confirms her process of spiritual growth and independence. All through childhood, she needed to hide her "core of being" from her narcissistic mother and violent father. Now, however, as this dream testifies, she has taken hold of her own core of being. Her next challenge will be to embrace that energy fully; only then will she be able to get to the animating spirit, which will lead her outward into creative life.

Despite her worries about the fragility of this hard-won growth, expressed as anxiety about messing up on the first day of her job, Grace has the benefit of her deep, dream-enhanced faith in God. Through the course of her therapeutic work with Bonnelle, she developed a personal rapport with the divine. She came to experience a vivid sense of God's presence in her life, in both waking and sleeping.

Ordinary Guy, Extraordinary Dreams

James is a writer who lives in a historic city on the southeastern seaboard of the United States. James and I are friends, and we have been sharing and talking about our dreams for several years.

He agreed that I could describe in this book his latest oneiric explorations. James's remarkable dreams have taught me new dimensions of the creativity of our sleeping minds, illustrating both the wonders and the challenges of spiritual dreaming.

James was born in Trinidad and Tobago to a family whose strict Catholicism coexisted uneasily with their ancestral roots in African spiritualities. From an early age, he was a vivid dreamer, as well as a persistent questioner of the religious teachings he received as a student at Catholic school. One of his aunts had a book about Greek myths, which she lent to James when he was twelve, and the book literally changed his life. He read it over and over again, absorbing the epic tales and vividly rendered stories and making them part of his imaginal world. James says he can still see the green cover of the book in his mind's eye.

When he came to the United States for college, his dreams began. Dreams of the divine, in a bewildering diversity of forms. Dreams about gods from the Greek pantheon, from Christianity, and from African traditions; dreams of numinous natural powers, wise ancestors, and interstellar journeys; dreams of gods from Hindu, Buddhist, and Nordic mythologies. And in all these dreams of his, who would you guess is the divine being who appears the most frequently—hundreds of times, according to James? If you accurately guess the identity of this special dream visitor, let me know, and I will dedicate my next book to you.

The answer is: the Hound of Hades. In my many years of experience in this field, I have never heard of *one*, let alone hundreds, of dreams of the three-headed dog Cerberus, but that's who James dreamed of. In Greek mythology, Cerberus serves as the Hound of Hades, guarding the gates to the underworld. Yet in James's dream life, Cerberus plays the role of an active companion as James moves through the dream world. Over the years, James has talked about his dreams at length with a psychotherapist, and he has also explored them in several dream-sharing groups. Thanks to these efforts, he has learned how to draw various kinds of meanings and insights from his dreams, which he appreciates. When he and I talk, however, his questions go beyond the possible meanings of particular dreams to reflect on the overall fact of his religiously charged dreaming. First and foremost, James wants to know: *Why me?* Why is he having—or perhaps receiving—so many vivid, intense dreams of gods, deities, and other religious beings?

The transcendent dreams of Kuiken's research are thought to occur only rarely, but James experiences these kinds of highly impactful, visually powerful dreams on a regular basis. James knows that other people actively seek out dreams like these, and they feel grateful if they have one or two transcendent dreams in their whole lives. Why are such dreams a constant feature of his oneiric experience? To be clear, James is a modest and self-effacing individual who is keenly aware of the dangers of ego inflation in these dreams. He says he feels like a regular person. In fact, far from taking any kind of credit for the dreams, James says they don't always feel like "his" dreams. It's as if they come from somewhere else, and he's just a receiver or filter. The visual intensity and religious symbolism of these dreams fill him with a vibrant sense of meaning, as would be found in a classic type of mystical experience (e.g., during meditation or prayer or in a waking vision). Like the mystics of Christianity, Buddhism, and other traditions, James struggles to express in ordinary language the plenitude of spiritual meanings coursing through his dreams.

The urgency James feels to understand these dreams stems from his second vital question: does he have a special responsibility to do something with the dreams? Having received what for many people would be a gift of tremendous value, he wonders how to respond. "What do I with this—with all these encounters?" he asked me once. What a strange dilemma he faces. As much as he felt called to share the dreams with others, James also knew from painful personal experience how dangerous it could be to share dreams in the wrong settings or with the wrong people. He had been ridiculed, teased, and shunned at various points in childhood because of his active and unruly imagination. Now, as a young Black man living in the US South, James is all too aware of the trouble his god-infused dreams could cause if he's not careful about where and with whom he talks about them.

This brief window into James's struggle—to understand why such an ordinary guy would have such extraordinary dreams— illustrates a hard truth about the life of a big dreamer: it can be lonely. Everyone has the potential for big, intense, influential dreams, but few people actualize that potential, and even fewer do so to the degree that James has. He and I have talked about how, if he had lived in a different time and place, his unusual capacity for divine dreaming would very likely have earned him unwanted attention from the religious and political authorities. And yet in still other historical or cultural contexts, his dreams might have been celebrated as a gift to the community, and he would have been honored as a wise seer and perhaps taken aside for special training as a shaman. Alas, in our collective reality of the early twenty-first century, he faces a social landscape uncomfortably closer to the former scenario than the latter. For James, the loneliness of having a special capacity for dreaming is compounded by social biases and anti-dream attitudes from his peers and from wider culture.

I can think of several possible explanations for James's unusual dream life. Maybe it's the result of his mixed cultural and religious background, or perhaps it was triggered by his sudden social dislocation. Perhaps it's an oedipal drama projected into the heavens or an anomaly in his neurological functioning. Or maybe that old green book of Greek myths just really did a number on him. Each of these explanations, even the last, probably has some merit. But all of them fall short too. Any explanation like these can be just one more attempt to reduce the dreams to another kind of process or activity, one that supposedly has more importance or occupies a more fundamental level of reality.

Dreams like the ones that James has shared with me seem to call for the opposite approach: rather than trying to explain them, shrink them down, or reduce them to something we quantify, we can try to expand our awareness to embrace their radical mystery and infinite unpredictability. The medium *is* the message. Instead of waiting for the dreams to provide us with answers like a magic eight-ball, we should revel in the exploration of their ever-expanding questions. The capacity even to ask such existentially profound questions represents a remarkable stage in the growth of consciousness, one that deserves to be celebrated for the exciting new horizons it opens up.

This is much easier to say than to do. I know from talking with James that he frequently bumps up against situations in the waking world where his highly reflective view of the world clashes with the conventional beliefs and behaviors of other people. He told me that twice in previous job situations, he had approached his supervisor with what he thought were respectful and well-reasoned suggestions about making changes to the overall system that would improve the quality and efficiency of everyone's work. In both cases, he was essentially told to mind his own business and leave well enough alone. James was surprised such obviously beneficial changes would be rejected out of hand. Yet he was not surprised to receive another confirmation of the drastic difference between his dream-infused perspective and the perspective of most other people.

James now splits his time between working in theater production and creative writing. Not knowing what else to suggest, I have encouraged him to write as a way of honoring his dreams and sharing their insights with others, which is where the dreams themselves seem to be moving. I honestly don't know why James has the dreams he does, but I'm quite sure he will do best if he regards his dreams of the gods as a spiritual gift rather than as a curse, or a random misfiring of his brain, or a symptom of psychopathology, or a narcissistic fantasy, or any other reductive explanation. By accepting these dreams as a spiritual gift, by conceiving of them in that metaphorical context, there is less emphasis on what to *do* with them and more encouragement to appreciate them and explore them. What if James—and all of us who even occasionally dream vivid, spiritually insightful dreams—could simply *be* with them?

The Shadow

Generally speaking, dreams have more negative content than positive content. They have more fear than happiness, more misfortunes than good fortunes, more falling than flying. They have more aggression than sexuality and more demons than gods. The content analysis category of "fantastic beings" is a grab bag of every character in the dream that is *not* a normal human or animal. Included in this category are monsters, vampires, fairies, ghosts, and aliens, along with humans and animals with supernatural powers (e.g., a witch, a wizard, or a flying pig). For most people, only 1 or 2 percent of their dreams have a reference to a fantastic being. And yet these dreams tend to be highly memorable and influential when they do occur.

Dreams of fantastic beings can represent one of the ways the archetype of the *shadow* appears in our lives. In Jungian psychology, archetypes are innate patterns of psychic energy that can be activated by important life experiences. The archetype of the shadow appears, Jung said, whenever the attitude of the conscious ego becomes too one-sided and overdeveloped in one direction. The frustration of these neglected mental potentials leads to the constellation of the shadow archetype, which represents everything left in the shadows of the unconscious. Jung drew on the universal metaphor of light and shadow to portray an imbalanced psychological relationship in which too much emphasis is put on the sunlit brightness of ego consciousness, leaving everything else in its shadow. In a way, the shadow is an archetype of the unconscious itself. It expresses that which is furthest from ego consciousness. It's the part of ourselves that feels the *least* like a part of ourselves and that perhaps we most wish were *not* a part of ourselves.

The shadow archetype plays a vital role in the practice of Jungian psychotherapy and in practices of spiritual formation too. For many people, this is the first archetype they recognize within themselves. It can mark a humbling first step toward a greater awareness of one's deepest fears and weaknesses and also of one's deepest potential for growth. The ultimate psychospiritual goal is a full integration of the shadow with the rest of the self, harmonizing its primal energies with a healthier ego and developing a more balanced conscious attitude toward the world. The path of integrating the shadow and moving toward what Jung called *individuation* has many obstacles, however.

The primary obstacle is the ego itself, which, not inaccurately, views the shadow as a threat to its sense of control and primacy in the mind. The more alienated consciousness becomes from the unconscious, the more monstrous the shadow will appear. Jung saw this as diagnostically important: the horribleness of a shadow figure indicates the degree to which a person has lost touch with their own inner depths.

The painful difficulty of coming to terms with the shadow is a common theme in the world's myths and literature, from ancient times to the present. We can observe shadow dynamics in many teachings about the devil through the centuries as the embodiment of those aspects of human life that the religious authorities of a given time have forbidden—for example, the seven deadly sins. In the classic Robert Louis Stevenson novella *The Strange Case of Dr. Jekyll and Mr. Hyde*—which was itself inspired by a dream—a scientific experiment gone awry transforms the mild-mannered Jekyll into the raging, murderous Hyde, revealing the hidden truth about his deepest nature. The original *King Kong* movie from 1933, one of my top three horror movies, involves an expedition of filmmakers to Skull Island, where the islanders have built an enormous wall to protect their small portion of dry land from the prehistoric monsters who roam the dense jungles on the other side, the greatest of which is the giant gorilla, Kong. The geography of Skull Island represents a roughly balanced mapping of the mind, and it is the folly of the filmmakers-within-the-film to assume they could capture Kong and bring him to New York as a spectacle. The shadow cannot be so easily contained.

The whole history of horror, fantasy, and science fiction, in fact, is filled with shadow figures—Gollum from J. R. R. Tolkien's *The Lord of the Rings* trilogy; the invading Martians from

H. G. Wells's *The War of the Worlds*; the fire-breathing, Tokyo-stomping Godzilla from the original 1954 film of the same name; and Freddy Krueger from the *A Nightmare on Elm Street* movies. You can probably think of shadow figures in other stories once you start looking for characters who embody the extreme negative values of their community. But these can be values the community actually needs if it is to solve its problems and grow into the future. According to Jung, the shadow always carries the seeds of light and growth, and it should be embraced for holding such potential, however difficult that embrace may be. The frightening monstrousness of the shadow reflects the ego's alienation and resistance toward the shadow—*not* the contents of the shadow itself.

I first learned of Jung's notion of the shadow during my initial teenage reading of books about dreams, and I quickly recognized this archetype in myself. I realized my personality was well developed in some areas but woefully underdeveloped in others; for instance, I had strong intellectual skills in waking life, but I had much less emotional self-awareness. In my dreams, I typically tried to use those intellectual skills to escape my pursuers, but it never worked. No idea was clever enough, no strategy smart enough, to get away. Most frustrating was my inability to reason or communicate with the monsters. They would not listen to my arguments, pleas, and negotiations. These nightmare figures seemed to consist of pure negative emotion.

As I began to reflect on these dreams as expressions of the shadow, I could see the antagonists as my own frustrated emotionality, which had no voice in my conscious life and which could only get my attention by repeated blasts of raw hostility via dreaming. And here's the thing: Once I realized this, and once I started trying to become more emotionally engaged with the world, *my dreams changed*. I still had scary dreams with shadow figures every now and then, but the recurrent loop of chasing nightmares stopped or at least morphed into a more varied and less pervasively negative dreamscape. Jung's notion of the shadow archetype gave me a name for something I had experienced but didn't understand. Once I had that name, I could begin to form a relationship with those alienated parts of myself and slowly move toward greater integration.

Although he developed it in his therapeutic work with individuals, Jung also used the concept of the shadow as a psychological explanation for social prejudices of various kinds—racial, religious, ethnic, and sexual, among others. According to Jung, an unhealthy but temporarily effective way of dealing with the shadow is to *project* it. In his view, social prejudices like racism, homophobia, and anti-Semitism are clear indicators of a deep inner split and lack of shadow integration. Instead of integrating the neglected parts of the psyche into ourselves, we project them outward onto other people, who then appear as the embodiment of everything evil, immoral, and abhorrent. The ego then tries to protect, justify, or legitimate its control of consciousness by increasingly harsh attacks on those with the misfortune to be on the receiving end of our projections. By attacking them, we seek to defend our own alienated self, and yet like a Chinese finger puzzle, the more we struggle against the shadow, the more tightly it grips us. Projecting the underdeveloped parts of one's psyche onto others doesn't really work, of course; it just dehumanizes other people and prevents our own real growth. But given the choice between integrating the shadow and projecting it onto others, all of us make the latter choice more often than we should.

The end of Jung's life saw the rise of the Cold War between the United States and the Soviet Union, and he used the shadow as a frame for understanding this polarizing political conflict that threatened the whole planet with nuclear annihilation. Here is how he put it in *Man and His Symbols*, one of the last things he wrote before he died in 1961: "It is the face of his own evil shadow that grins at Western man from the other side of the Iron Curtain." This could be said of any kind of prejudice: that it holds up a brutally honest mirror, showing what we most fear about ourselves. Could dreaming help us develop greater self-awareness about our own prejudices, more than is normally possible in the waking state alone?

Everyone is a dreamer, and everyone has the innate power to envision transcendent insights with tremendous value for their community. This is the basic dream-infused faith that can help us look past all the apparent differences that divide us and appreciate the profound dreamer in each and every human being. The history of religions and modern neuroscience agree on this singular, amazing point: we are all dreamers.

The Shadow's Shadow

One of the greatest artistic portrayals of a shadow—a demonically "Other" figure—is the character Caliban in William Shakespeare's play *The Tempest*. Written and first performed sometime around 1610, *The Tempest* was the last major play Shakespeare wrote. The story centers on the ill-fated adventures of the powerful magician Prospero. Betrayed by his brother and exiled from his dukedom of Milan, Prospero and his infant daughter, Miranda, wash ashore on an enchanted island inhabited by no other humans, only a host of whimsical nature spirits, plus one other creature—Caliban. Caliban's mother, a witch exiled to this island years earlier, spawned him after mating with the devil.

When Prospero and Miranda arrive, Caliban is forced to yield the island to them and serve as their slave.

Prospero and Caliban have a terrible relationship, fraught with violent tension. Prospero torments Caliban mercilessly, sending spirits to pinch and prick him all over his body for the slightest misbehavior. Caliban, meanwhile, swears profusely at Prospero: "You taught me language, and my profit on't is, I know how to curse." Caliban had previously tried to rape Miranda, and during the play, he conspires with others to murder Prospero: "I'll yield him thee asleep, where thou mayest knock a nail into his head." In psychological terms, the relationship between Prospero and Caliban reflects a severely unhealthy balance between ego and shadow, with the former acting as an arrogant monarch and the latter as a blind force of resentful anarchy. They seem forever stuck in their dysfunctional bond.

And yet, in one of the most unexpectedly beautiful passages of the play, Caliban speaks of his own dreams:

Be not afeard; the isle is full of noises,
Sounds and sweet airs that give delight and hurt not.
Sometimes a thousand twanging instruments
Will hum about mine ears; and sometime voices
That, if I then had waked after long sleep,
Will make me sleep again; and then, in dreaming,
The clouds methought would open and show riches
Ready to drop upon me, that, when I waked,
I cried to dream again.

This sweetly mournful speech of Caliban's answers a question that perceptive readers of Jung will eventually ask. If the shadow of a proper, civilized person like Dr. Jekyll takes the form of a monstrous Mr. Hyde, then what is the shadow like for a person who, in their waking life, acts upon their violent, aggressive, egocentric desires? What is the shadow of a shadow?

According to Jung, people like that will have dreams of the *light shadow*, reminding them of their underdeveloped capacities for compassion, kindness, and joy. Caliban seems to experience something like that with his dreams of the clouds opening above him and showering down riches. No matter how horribly vicious and cruel his waking behavior, Caliban still has the deep unconscious potential for more positive and life-affirming aspects of himself to emerge.

Prospero is not onstage when Caliban relates his dreams. Thus, at the end of the play when Prospero famously says of Caliban, "This thing of darkness I acknowledge mine," it comes across as a grudging acceptance of the shadow rather than a welcoming embrace. But we in the audience know more than Prospero does about Caliban's higher spiritual potential. This is the gift of the play. It brings us to a place where we can envision an even greater integration than these two characters can recognize themselves. Even though it is merely fiction, the play gives us a glimpse of a higher spiritual dream. It envisions a move toward more respect for all dreamers, no matter how shadowy or monstrous we may at first assume them to be.

CHAPTER 6

Visitations from Beyond
Death and Dying

My mother began her work as a hospice chaplain while I was in graduate school. When a person with a terminal illness entered hospice care and asked to talk with someone about religious or spiritual concerns, hospice would try to bring in someone with whom the patient already had a relationship: the patient's priest, rabbi, pastor, or some other clergyperson. But if the dying person had no such prior relationship and yet needed to talk about the many questions, worries, and uncertainties filling their minds, my mother stepped in.

Every time she entered a hospice patient's room, she felt she truly had no idea what to expect. Some of the people without any religious background were now consumed with urgent spiritual questions. Others had grown up in a faith tradition but then drifted away from it as adults, leaving them with the equivalent of kindergarten theology to help them face death. A few were highly religious people who couldn't talk honestly with anyone else about their sudden loss of belief in God just at the time when they most wanted the consolations of faith. Mostly, the people she encountered were scared. They were also angry, and sad, and confused, and often in some degree of pain. Some felt overwhelmed by regrets and despair; life already seemed done and over, and death was just the final formality.

My mother's chaplaincy practice centered on sitting, listening, and being a companion for people at this singular moment of their lives. She let the conversation unfold at its own pace, and she waited for an opportunity to ask if the person would like to pray or meditate together, or read some passages from a special book, or arrange for a meeting with a friend or family member.

At some point, my mother also began asking if the person had experienced any dreams or visions recently. This question stemmed in part from my studies of dreams, which intrigued her and which she thought might be helpful in her caregiving efforts. She quickly found that many of her hospice patients were frequent and vivid dreamers. More than that, several of them had visions in their waking state, with feelings, images, and themes very similar to those of their dreams. Not everyone had such experiences, but a surprisingly large number of her patients did, and she soon realized that predeath dreams and visions have important implications for end-of-life care. "If you happen to hear one of these dreams, consider yourself blessed," she would say later. "You might have just been given a rare insight into the world to come."

People living in modern Western societies hold ambivalent and inconsistent attitudes around death, mostly trying to avoid it or not look at it. As anthropologist Ernest Becker observed years ago, we are a culture in "denial of death." Yet my mother's experiences showed that those who are dying still retain their essential humanity, including the capacity to dream. Dying is not simply an end but rather a new chapter of life, with its own dynamics and opportunities. In her teaching and writing, in her sermons and public talks, and in her one-on-one conversations with hospice patients, my mother exemplified spiritual leadership in an area of tremendous community need.

Anyone who decides to pay attention to their dreams will encounter the theme of death and dying sooner or later—and probably sooner. Long before your physical body expires, your unconscious psyche is anticipating death, preparing for it, and imagining what comes next. This chapter will give you several ways to understand references to death, dying, and loss in dreams. I will share some ideas from a book my mother and I wrote together, *Dreaming beyond Death*, which focuses on the spiritual potentials in predeath dreams and visions, using Lakoff's ideas about metaphor to develop a practical approach to the interpretation of these special kinds of dreams. We will also consider the nearly universal occurrence of visitation dreams, in which someone who is dead appears as if alive. Such dreams play an important role in people's beliefs about the soul and the afterlife, and they can provide invaluable emotional reassurance in times of deep sadness and mourning.

The Tribe of Dreams

The human mythic imagination has long connected our experiences of sleep, dreaming, and death. In the Western tradition, this relationship appears in one of the oldest sacred texts of ancient Greece, the *Theogony* of Hesiod, from the eighth century BCE, almost three thousand years ago. *Theogony* can be roughly translated as "the genealogy of the gods," meaning it tells the story of how the gods themselves came into being and how their family tree branched out over time. In Hesiod's poetic rendering of this tale, before the appearance of the Olympian deities like Zeus and Athena and before the appearance of the chthonic titans like Chronos and Gaia, an even earlier group of primordial beings emerged. These gods, Hesiod wrote, would shape the reality of everyone who came after: "And Night bore frightful Doom and the black Ker, and Death, and Sleep, and the whole tribe of Dreams."

We don't know who or what "the black Ker" refers to, but if its siblings include Death and frightful Doom, it can't be good. And yet Sleep is a sibling too, a genuine child of the Night. The ancient Greeks knew of the vital restorative qualities of slumber, so this suggests that Night's all-embracing domain is not unremittingly grim. Sleep, although surrounded on all sides by supremely frightening cosmic monsters, offers humans a safe haven in a very dangerous world.

And what of the "whole tribe of Dreams"? I love this image, which suggests a multiplicity that comes together into a rough but powerful unity. We might expect that Sleep and Dreams would emerge from Night, but their connection to Death may not be so apparent. In ancient Greek culture, and in many cultures around the world, a dream is believed to involve the disembodied soul of the individual either journeying to other realms or receiving visits from other disembodied souls. This is why many linguistic traditions speak of "seeing" rather than "having" a dream. For the ancient Greeks and many other people, dreams involve real encounters with autonomous beings who are not simply the products of our limited human minds. These beings expand our minds and connect us to greater networks of meaning and intelligence. This means, however, that when we are asleep and dreaming, we are, for all intents and purposes, dead. Motionless, unresponsive, inert: from the outside, it appears the only things that distinguishes sleep from death are breath and the ability to wake up. To sleep without waking is perhaps the most common poetic euphemism for death.

The connection between dreaming and death plays an important role in Tibetan Buddhism, where many ritual and meditation practices revolve around preparing the soul for death and the transitional process to a newly incarnated existence. If you have led a good life in this existence and the preparations are successful, you will be reborn in a form further along the path toward ultimate enlightenment. The *Bardo Thodol*, a fourteenth-century CE text known in the West as the *Tibetan Book of the Dead*, provides the core teachings on these practices, and it includes dreaming as one of the *bardos*, or intermediate states of consciousness, that can be cultivated into spiritual resources for approaching death and rebirth. In this spiritual tradition, dreaming provides a kind of practice for death, a way of getting ready for the real thing.

The present-day Dalai Lama, leader of the contemporary Tibetan Buddhist community, shared essentially the same views with a group of Western researchers, which were then published in the book *Sleeping, Dreaming, and Dying: An Exploration of Consciousness with the Dalai Lama*. He, too, emphasizes the importance of preparing for death by means of carefully cultivating a higher degree of self-awareness and nonattachment during all states of consciousness. As a reward, we may receive an inspiring hint of what a more fully actualized and enlightened self might feel like: "In the Tibetan Buddhist literature, it is said that one experiences a glimpse of clear light on various occasions, including sneezing, fainting, dying, sexual intercourse, and sleep," he says. "Normally, our sense of self, or ego, is quite strong and we tend to relate to the world with that subjectivity. But on these particular occasions, this strong sense of self is slightly relaxed."

The Dalai Lama puts his finger on a key point of connection between dreaming and death. They both involve a severe reduction in the centralized control of the ego—temporarily in the former, permanently in the latter. Dreaming provides a powerful source of spiritual preparation for death precisely because it involves a surrender of ordinary ego consciousness and a radical openness to other dimensions of the self and reality.

A little-known testament to the spiritual value of dreaming in Christianity's teachings about death appears in a letter written by Augustine of Hippo, the great theologian from the fourth century CE. Augustine was replying to a friend who had asked him about dreams and the soul's existence after death. In the letter, Augustine describes a dream experience of someone he knew, a man named Gennadius, who had also been wondering about the afterlife. In the dream, a young man asks Gennadius a series of questions about the relationship between his sleeping body and his dreaming soul, questions that Gennadius realizes he cannot answer. At the end of this Socratic dialogue, the young man reveals the truth toward which he has been leading the confused dreamer:

> As while you are asleep and lying on your bed these eyes of your body are now unemployed and doing nothing, and yet you have eyes with which you behold me, and enjoy this vision, so, after your death, while your bodily eyes shall be wholly inactive, there shall be in you a life by which you shall still live, and a faculty of perception by which you shall still perceive. Beware, therefore, after this of harboring doubts as to whether the life of man shall continue after death.

In this story, the experience of dreaming provides a direct model for the experience of death. Just as we see, feel, and think in our dreams without regard to our sleeping bodies, so shall our immortal souls continue to see, feel, and think after death without regard to our lifeless bodies. Augustine asks his friend, "By whom was he [Gennadius] taught this but by the merciful, providential care of God?" As a pastor seeking to comfort a member of his flock, Augustine encourages his friend to think about the compassionate spirituality of death-related dreams, how they provide us with powerful, divinely reassuring visions of our soul's journey beyond the bounds of death. Many centuries later, Augustine's advice still rings true: people today still experience intense spiritual dreams about death, dying, and the dead. The difference is that modern secular society does little to prepare people for such dreams. Thanks to my mother and others who work in palliative care, that may be changing.

The Journey Ahead

The *Dreaming beyond Death* book I cowrote with my mother, Patricia, began as her doctoral of ministry thesis at Princeton Theological Seminary. Having gathered her observations and insights from several years of hospice work, she had written an excellent study of the recurrent themes in, and practical insights to be gained from, predeath dreams and visions. I encouraged her in the project and, when she finished, suggested she develop it into a book. She said she would but only if I helped her. So together we framed what she had learned in terms that a broad audience could understand and appreciate.

Her years of caring for hospice patients had led her to recognize an overarching theme in virtually all of their spiritual experiences: the metaphor of *death as a journey*. In dreams, the journey metaphor appeared so frequently that my mother began to anticipate and welcome its appearance. She found that each predeath dream is unique, playing out the journey metaphor in its own particular way and according to an individual's life circumstances. Yet by collecting a large number of predeath dreams from many people and sorting through the recurrent themes and images, as she did for her thesis, we can identify a few clusters of journey-related content. Later in this chapter, we will explore how these metaphorical themes appear in specific dreams. Here I will simply highlight what we see in predeath dreams.

If death is conceived as a journey, it implies a movement, by some means, from one place to another, and predeath dreams tend to involve familiar modes of transportation. In my mother's collection, she had gathered dreams of people traveling in cars, boats, trains, and on foot; crossing bridges, streams, and oceans; moving up, down, and horizontally. In addition to transportation, the dreamers often set out on their journeys with the assistance of a guide. In most cases, the guide is a well-known, familiar, trustworthy person who has already died and now has come back to help the dreamer make the same transition. Guiding figures include parents and grandparents, teachers and friends, even children and animals if they have predeceased the dreamer.

The third cluster of predeath dream content she found involves obstacles along the journey. The obstacles can be as literal as a huge boulder or broken bridge or more abstract, like a painful secret or a lost friendship. Predeath dreams involving obstacles, although painful for the individual, can be very helpful to caregivers in identifying issues they can address to help the person approach death with as much dignity and comfort as possible.

The overall impact of predeath dreams and visions tended to be quite positive and sometimes dramatically so. The dying person's attitude toward death often changes as a result of the dream, from fear and despair toward a reassuring sense of readiness or even anticipation. Not everyone in my mother's practice experienced these effects, but a significant number of them did—enough that it made her wonder how many other people approaching death, in hospice or otherwise, were having—or seeing—dreams that could help them better prepare for the end of their lives.

The big obstacle here, she realized, is the modern healthcare system itself, which does little to prepare doctors, nurses, and other caregivers for the near-inevitability of such dreams when people approach death. Meaningful improvements in the emotional and spiritual well-being of hospice patients can be made with just the slightest adjustment of treatment practices—allowing patients to get undisturbed sleep, making sure not to overmedicate them, and periodically asking them open-ended questions about their dreams and anything else they might be seeing, hearing, or feeling. None of this requires accepting or promoting any specific theological belief or religious doctrine about the soul and the afterlife. It simply means being a compassionate, humane presence during a supremely mysterious process that we cannot fully understand—until, that is, the time comes for our own journey to the farthest edges of dreaming and beyond.

Later researchers have developed these insights and performed more systematic research than was possible within my mother's hospice practice. Foremost among these researchers is Christopher Kerr, a medical doctor in Buffalo specializing in hospice and palliative care. In a 2014 paper, he and his colleagues reported on an in-depth study involving sixty-six patients admitted to a hospice inpatient unit, focusing on their end-of-life dreams and visions (ELDVs). Here is their summary of their findings:

> Most participants reported experiencing at least one dream/vision. Almost half of the dreams/visions occurred while asleep, and nearly all patients indicated that they felt real. The most common dreams/visions included deceased friends/relatives and living friends/relatives. Dreams/visions featuring the deceased (friends, relatives, and animals/pets) were significantly more comforting than those of the living, living and deceased combined, and other people and experiences. As participants approached death, comforting dreams/visions of the deceased became more prevalent. ELDVs are commonly experienced phenomena during the dying process, characterized by a consistent sense of realism and marked emotional significance. These dreams/visions may be a profound source of potential meaning and comfort for the dying, and therefore warrant clinical attention and further research.

Kerr and his colleagues have performed several other studies, increasing our awareness of the beneficial impact of these kinds of dreams for the dying—and potentially for the living too. Once you realize how frequently people who are approaching death experience dreams and visions like this, you can put this knowledge to good use whenever you find yourself in a caregiving position. You don't have to wait for the person to bring up a dream; you can go ahead and ask. An invitation to dreamsharing can be a precious gift for someone facing the end of their life by helping them make their final times with loved ones as rich and meaningful as possible.

When the Dead Come Back

After a person has died, they may appear again to the living in their dreams. As with everything dream-related, there is no easy way to predict or stimulate such dreams, which researchers refer to as *visitation dreams*. Some people wish fervently they could have the consolation of a dream reunion with a deceased loved one. Other people, though, feel plagued by recurrent dreams of the dead person coming back in distress or with a warning or criticism.

It appears that nearly half the US adult population has experienced at least one visitation dream in their lives. Survey research I've done with the SDDb reveals this. Significantly, this category of dream is the only "typical" dream with a higher frequency of occurrence among older people than younger people. With all other typical dreams—such as flying, being chased, engaging in sexual activities—younger people have much higher frequencies. But when it comes to being visited in a dream by someone who has already died, our dreaming seems to become more open the older we get. Then again, if death strikes a close family member when we are young, the impact on dreaming can be immediate and intense.

A student once sought me out for advice about some recurrent dreams (he agreed that I could share his dream using a pseudonym). Manuel's grandmother died when he was thirteen years old. His grandmother, whom he called Nana, was originally from a small village in the desert hills of Mexico, and Manuel always remembered her as being the center of emotional power in their large, close-knit family. Whenever Manuel got sick, his mother would take him to Nana, and she would perform a traditional ritual to restore his health, whispering prayers in Spanish and rubbing a potion made of herbs, oils, egg, and ash all over him. Everyone in the family treated Nana with the greatest of respect out of awe for her deep wisdom and also, Manuel knew, out of fear of Nana's anger when she was crossed.

The terrible sense of loss Manuel felt when Nana died got worse when his older relatives had bitter arguments over her money and possessions. The family split into several angry factions, and for years afterward, Manuel was haunted by memories of the old family parties and holiday gatherings that were so much fun when Nana was still alive. When Manuel finished high school, he went to a prestigious university on the East Coast. He was the first member of his family to go to college, and as graduation approached, he wished Nana could come back and be a part of the ceremony.

One night during his senior year of college, Manuel had this dream:

> It's my college graduation, but the ceremony is in the hall where my high school baseball banquets were held, so it feels like home. A big crowd of people are there conversing, and I see a few family members, but I hear nothing. I see people's mouths moving and realize that people are understanding each other, but no words can be heard. Next, I look toward the entrance of the hall and see some of my great-uncles entering the hall. Following them is my Nana, who is followed by my great-aunt. They are all walking directly toward my family and me. Suddenly, I am overcome with good feelings.

I feel no worries, no tension at all. Everybody is just happy. My eyes lock with my Nana's eyes, and I experience extreme feelings of joy and happiness. Everything is still mute, but she is communicating to me that she is very proud. All of a sudden I see my Nana with her back to the floor. I am on my knees right beside her, with my arm supporting her neck and my left hand caressing one of her hands. I have a weird feeling, and I look up and sense that everyone is in a state of pandemonium. I see complete panic on my family's faces. I hear nothing, but I can tell by their faces that they are thinking that they need an ambulance and that they are fearing for Nana's life. But I just keep thinking that everything is all good. I look back at Nana's face, and I see in her eyes that she is telling me not to worry, that everything is fine. I know I don't have anything to worry about, and I communicate to her that yes, I understand. Everyone else is still panicking. Inside I feel nothing but complete bliss, and as I look at my Nana, I am 100 percent sure that she is at peace with herself. Everybody needs to relax!

At this point, Manuel suddenly woke up, filled with those same incredible feelings of joy and contentment. He smiled and actually laughed out loud. He said that as he lay in bed, he felt "an absolute happiness flowing throughout all parts of my body." The feelings were so vivid that they stayed with him for the rest of the day. At a rational level, Manuel did not have a simple explanation for what he had experienced. But he remembered Nana had always said that when she died, she would come back to people in their dreams to make sure they continued behaving well. Maybe his dream showed that Nana's soul was indeed still alive and had actually come back to him, just as she said she would, to guide him in a time of need. Or maybe his dreams simply reflected his own deep unconscious desire to have Nana back in his life, a desire so strong that it generated this remarkable dream experience. Manuel wasn't sure, and he couldn't with certainty rule out either possibility.

Whatever its final explanation, Manuel's dream became a valuable source of emotional strength as he tried to bring his fractured family back together. At the beginning of the dream, Manuel's family is part of the friendly but anonymous crowd, speaking in a way that Manuel is not able to hear. He can't follow what they are talking about because he is evidently tuned into an entirely different mode of perception. Suddenly his Nana and several other deceased relatives come into the auditorium. Manuel and Nana "lock eyes" and silently, without using words, begin sharing their thoughts and feelings with each other. Then the scene abruptly shifts, and Nana is on the floor, with Manuel holding her. The rest of the family panics, fearing that Nana is dying. But the special connection Manuel has with Nana remains strong and clear. Deep down, he knows Nana is fine.

There is no cowardly denial of Nana's dying in this dream, no wish-fulfilling fantasy of her getting off the floor and returning to normal life. What Manuel discovers in the dream is a profound confidence that even though Nana is leaving him, they will still be together. The rest of the family cannot see beyond Nana's death; they cannot perceive anything other than the pain of separation. Manuel now understands what the rest of his family does not: that even after Nana has died, a mysterious but incredibly powerful emotional connection will remain. Manuel's dream reveals to him the deeply paradoxical truth of this living connection beyond Nana's physical death. Even though he could not explain his dream, he now knew, with an absolute and unshakeable certainty, that he could continue following Nana's guidance and do his best to remind his family of her continuing influence on all of them.

Visitation dreams like Manuel's have always stimulated spiritual reflection because they involve a vivid and extremely realistic encounter between the dreamer and someone who is no longer of this world. These dreams stand out because the dead person appears more alive, animated, and self-possessed than characters usually appear in our dreams. "It felt like my grandma [or spouse, parent, child] was really there": that's a common reaction people have to such dreams. As in Manuel's case, the dreamer is often the only one to see or communicate with the dead person, who has returned to provide the dreamer with guidance, reassurance, and perhaps an important warning. Visitation dreams have a tremendous emotional impact on people—sometimes so great that the images and sensations remain clear and distinct in their memories years later.

Touched

Many visitation dreams culminate in the dreamer enjoying one last hug or touch from the person who has died. In the midst of the embrace, the dreamer focuses special attention on the quality of the dead person's body and the physical sensations of their touching each other. Another former student of mine, a thirty-four-year-old woman I'll call Ruth, told me about a dream she had in the wake of her mother's death. Her mother had been diagnosed with brain cancer, and while her doctors did everything they could, the cancer spread quickly. In just a matter of weeks, she died. Ruth and her family were devastated by the horrible and sudden loss of the woman who had always been the center of the family. Three months after her mother's death, Ruth had this dream:

> I am at my family's house, and I hear some noise upstairs, the wind blowing a door open and shut. I call, "Mom, is that you?" and I hear the door open and shut twice, as if in response. Then I am in the kitchen, and I see Mom's slippers on the floor, moving toward me. Mom slowly materializes up from her slippers and reaches out to me. Her eyes are closed at first, and she slowly struggles to open them. I am terrified, but I do not run. I let Mom hug me, and her body feels strange, thin and kind of soft. I ask her how she is doing, and she says, "It's good, it's good," over and over. I want to ask more questions, but I realize Mom won't give me any more answers. Finally, she says she must go and tells me she can come back one more time. Mom hugs me, and I wake up hugging myself.

Ruth called this "one of the 'realest' experiences of my life, a dream unlike any of the others I've had of Mom since she died." When Ruth awoke from the dream, she found herself tightly hugging her own body. She couldn't help thinking that her mother had really been there—the physical power was so different from any other she had experienced. And yet Ruth knew that the paradoxical meaning of the dream was that her mother was really gone too: "I realize Mom won't give me any more answers."

In some visitation dreams, the physicality of the encounter takes on an almost clinical quality. Thirty-two-year-old Kim, the pseudonym for an attendee at a workshop I once led, went with a group of friends to visit their old college roommate Keith, who had been stricken with cancer and was near death. Kim was overwhelmed by the horrifying sight of her good friend lying in the hospital's intensive care unit, heavily sedated and hooked up to life-support machines. From his hospital bed, Keith was able to hear Kim and the others when they spoke to him, but he could respond to them only through a machine that beeped at each reaction. After they left the hospital, Kim realized with a stab of regret that she had forgotten to hold Keith's hand one last time. She had been so overcome with emotion that she never physically touched him. A week later, Keith died, and that night Kim had a dream:

> I am lying in my bed when I see Keith at my bedside and feel the warmth of his skin as he slowly reaches for my hand. He stands close to me and holds my hand gently yet firmly for a long time. This feeling of his hand against mine is so real, too real to be a dream. In addition to the warmth of his flesh, I feel the firmness and thickness of his hand and the wrinkles that form on his palm and fingers as he holds my hand. Neither of us speak, nor is there any sound in the dream, and the atmosphere is that of tranquility.

When Kim awoke, the sense of touching Keith was still in her hand. She couldn't believe it was possible to have such an intensely realistic physical sensation without actually having held another person's hand in her own. Kim was generally a skeptic regarding the supernatural; her work as a high school biology teacher gave her a strong appreciation for reason, logic, and science. Although she didn't think her dream proved that ghosts or spirits exist, she admitted that she had never had such an experience before. In fact, she even hesitated to call it a dream because it was so uniquely realistic and vivid. She felt that somehow or other, Keith had really come back and that he was trying to ease her regrets about that last sad visit to the hospital. In the dream, their positions are reversed—now Kim is the one lying motionless in bed, and Keith is standing beside her. Then he does what Kim wished she had done: he reaches for her hand and takes it in his own for a final, wordless goodbye.

When Kim woke up, she saw that Keith was gone. Slowly, she remembered that yesterday he had died, but now his touch still lingered in her hand. As Kim lay in bed, she knew she would never forget this feeling of having really been with him one last time.

Death as a Metaphor

Not all dreams of death are literally about someone dying. Most of the time, death-related dreams are metaphorical in their meaning and significance. The supreme existential importance of death makes it a perfect metaphor for dreams to use in conveying a variety of meanings. When people suffer especially dire losses or find themselves going through painful periods of change, metaphorical dreams of death often emerge to bring to full awareness deep feelings about what they are experiencing. Just like dreams in which sexuality serves as a symbol to express nonsexual meanings, these dreams use dramatic, attention-grabbing images of death and dying to symbolize other kinds of serious concerns.

One night during her sophomore year in college, Rita, a former student who discussed this dream with me over several meetings, had a terribly frightening dream that her father had died. The dream's setting jumped from place to place, but what Rita remembered most clearly was being at her high school football field, where, in waking life, she and her classmates had gathered for graduation:

> I am at my father's funeral. I am supposed to give a speech for him, with hundreds of people sitting in white chairs on the field before me. I start talking, but midway through my talk the people in the chairs start filing off the field row by row. I keep going with the speech anyway, and when I am finished, my mother pulls me aside and says, "It was only supposed to be a penny!" Although this phrase doesn't seem to fit the situation, I know that my mom means I was only supposed to talk for one minute. Then I am pounding on the kitchen floor of my boyfriend's home, screaming "It's not fair!" over and over again.

When she woke up, Rita was in tears, and she couldn't sleep for the rest of the night. First thing in the morning, she called her father to make sure he was all right—she feared her dream might mean he was really going to die. To her relief, her father was fine, and after their conversation, Rita was left to ponder the meaning of her deeply affecting but evidently not predictive dream. As she thought about it, she realized that in addition to feeling sad, she also felt angry and frustrated because there was nothing she could do to change or fix the situation. The recurrent cry of "It's not fair!" echoed in her mind as a poignant expression of deep, raw emotion.

And why had she seemed to be the only person grieving? No one else at the funeral expressed any feelings. Rita was especially struck by the coldness of her mother's criticism for exceeding the proper time in her funeral speech. The strange words her mother used—"It was only supposed to be a penny!"—had a demeaning and hurtful tone. In addition, several friends and family members in the dream ask Rita how her father had died; to her intense frustration, her dream self doesn't know how to answer them. The fact that in her dream her father's cause of death was unknown led Rita to try to think of a more symbolic or metaphorical way of understanding the dream. She found herself thinking about how in waking life, she missed seeing her father on a regular basis. As Rita focused on these feelings of sadness and loss, the various elements of the dream began to make sense.

Her parents had separated two years earlier, during the summer following her high school graduation. As a result, Rita's father had moved to a different town, and he and Rita could not see each other as much as they had in the past. The night before the dream, Rita and her mother had argued about the separation, which seemed to be the basis for their strange interaction about the funeral speech. Although Rita had struggled over the preceding two years to hide her grief, in the dream, she finally let loose with her real emotions, despite the crowd's inattention and her mother's dismissive words. Rita's high school graduation was the last time she remembered her family being together and happy, in stark contrast to the atmosphere of tragic sadness in the dream. She said to me, "I believe the dream was telling me that I need to find a balance in my life, in which I let go of what I can't change and make the best out of what I have." Although she did not lose her dad physically, she realized she had lost him in other ways, that he had metaphorically "died." She now knew the time had come for her to accept that fact and move on.

The understanding that Rita gradually reached about her dream highlights an important element in dreams of death: Death is always the beginning of new life. This element is often lost amid the overwhelming feelings of sadness and loss. But if one reflects carefully enough on the dream, a ray of hope almost always arises, a reason to continue having faith in the future. The eternal cycle of life, death, and rebirth that governs nature also governs our emotional lives. Dreams like Rita's illustrate how any experience of loss, no matter how tragic or devastating, creates the opportunity for new life and new growth.

After her high school graduation, Rita went to college and met new friends, enjoyed her studies, and learned how to live on her own. Although her dream made her more aware of her deep hurt over the loss of her father, she also felt encouraged by the dream to move forward in her life. The spiritual paradox of the cycle of life, death, and rebirth emerges in this painful but necessary process. Only by fully accepting the reality of a terrible emotional loss can new life begin to take form and to grow into the future.

Companions at the Threshold

The oneiric experiences of these individuals bring them to the borderlands between the living and the dead, where they gain insights into the well-being of deceased loved ones and make peace with the ultimate finitude of their lives. For some people, visitation dreams come as a surprise or even a shock. If your culture has not prepared you for it, the vivid appearance of a dead person in a dream can appear as a destabilizing rupture in the natural order. A great deal of fear and misunderstanding surrounds dreams of death, dying, and the dead. Here is another cultural space where big dreamers can make a truly important and meaningful contribution to community well-being. As indicated by my mother's hospice work, a few simple practices can yield valuable results. Just raising the topic among people who are mourning a loved one's death, or among medical staff in hospital palliative care units, can have potentially huge spiritual effects.

A good friend and expert in this realm of dream exploration is Jeanne Van Bronkhorst, author of *Dreams at the Threshold*. Jeanne also has extensive experience in caregiving for people with terminal illnesses in Canada, and her findings correspond closely to what my mother found in a primarily US context—the recurrent journey patterns in predeath dreams and visions, their hyperrealism, their spiritual value, and their profoundly reassuring impact on the dreamer. Unfortunately, Jeanne has also found similar obstacles and barriers to recognizing the implications for improving hospice treatment.

Everyone who does actual in-person work with hospice patients knows those patients are seeing and hearing things, both awake and asleep, that no one else in the room can perceive. And yet little or nothing is done to acknowledge the supreme spiritual importance of these experiences to the patient. Here is how Jeanne puts it:

> Talk to any long-term care staff and you will find stories of such unusual one-sided conversations. It is not uncommon for them to walk into a patient's room and find that person speaking with or watching people they themselves can't see. Some patients might speak of the vivid presence of people they love who are right there in the room, giving messages of love and encouragement. . . . In my early years as a hospital social worker, I walked in on enough of these moments to feel their emotional power. I would enter a person's hospital

room feeling confident in my professional role only to see the patient reluctantly turn her eye away from the ceiling or the window or empty chair to focus on me— polite but distant, as if I had just interrupted something beyond my comprehension.

Does this sound familiar? Like anything we have discussed earlier? The mainstream medical profession appears, to me, just as reluctant to recognize the imaginal experiences of hospice patients as zoologists are about recognizing the imaginal experiences of animals. In these instances, a bias against dreaming provides an excuse for denying others their own intrinsic and authentic subjectivity, their own phenomenal selfhood, their dignity and moral standing as conscious beings.

These issues have taken a painfully personal turn in the past couple of years. My mother's dementia has worsened to the point where she has lost much of her ability to verbalize her thoughts and feelings. She still retains, at least for now, a higher degree of receptive awareness, especially around emotionally important relationships (family, friends, cats). We can tell her stories from years ago, and she can say and gesture just enough to make it clear she's tracking with the memory. The significant downside to her current condition is that she has a great deal of awareness of her declining mental abilities, which can lead, in the worst moments, to a frightening kind of "locked-in" sensation. I know that many other families have similar and also much tougher experiences with Alzheimer's disease, and my heart goes out to any of you who are dealing with this kind of situation. It's a terrible way to lose a loved one. With my mother, the sad irony is that just as she approaches the end of her own life, all the knowledge and wisdom she developed over a lifetime of caregiving have become elusive to her. It's now my responsibility, and my honor, to bear that wisdom for her. To be honest, I knew this day was coming when we were writing the book, almost twenty years ago. I knew that at some level, we were preparing for this moment, whatever form it would take.

And my mother's spiritual interests in this time have taken a curious form indeed. In her periodic moments of clarity and focused energy, the thing my mom likes to do with me is read passages from *Tales of the Hasidim*, a collection of brief, vivid stories about the irreverent Hasidic rabbis of eighteenth- and nineteenth-century Eastern Europe. My mother was an ordained Presbyterian minister, and she has no Jewish familial background whatsoever. Yet she absolutely delights in these tricksterish tales of mystical Judaism, gathered and translated by the great theologian Martin Buber (author of the beautiful and highly influential *I and Thou*). I'm still trying to understand what she finds so compelling about these stories. She once told me that although she is a Christian, she gets fed up with the Christian church, and since Jesus was originally a Jewish mystic, perhaps the time had come to learn more about these deeper spiritual roots of her faith. That makes it sound awfully serious, however. As we read and discuss these stories, it's precisely the light, playful, nonintellectual aspects of the tales that engage her so much. Many of the tales turn on the Hasidim showing how a truly intimate relation with God can only emerge with the paradoxical rejection of conventional ideas, behaviors, rules, and morals. The Hasidim are constantly falling into trances, blurting out strange prayers and awkward prophecies, ignoring authorities, defying expectations, embracing irrationality, enjoying their bodily appetites, dreaming strange dreams, socializing with the dead, rhapsodizing about primordial sparks of light, laughing, crying, and dancing. This is what my mom loves: the exuberant, uninhibited spiritual freedom of the

Hasidim, their joyful embrace of God in every moment of their lives, and their refusal to be bound by merely human conventions in their wholehearted devotion to the divine.

At one point, I shared my mom's story with David Nirenberg, an eminent Jewish theologian and the former dean of the University of Chicago Divinity School. I asked him if he could tell me anything helpful about Buber's collection of stories and the many strange legends revolving around the Hasidim. He smiled and said that Buber's lyrical tales offer "infinite depths of projection." I immediately understood what he meant, or at least I think I did. *Infinite depths of projection*: those were his words. Of course, my mom loved his comment when I told her about it. It's a deeply evocative and memorable phrase and an apt way of expressing what brings my mother (and me) so much spiritual delight and levity as the darkening clouds gather ever closer.

Part III

Aspirations

CHAPTER 7

Lucid: Dreaming to Expand Consciousness

"When one goes to sleep, he takes along the material of this all-containing world, himself tears it apart, himself builds it up, and dreams by his own brightness, by his own light," says the *Brihadaranyaka Upanishad*, a classic source of Hindu wisdom about spiritual dreaming from the sixth century BCE. "Then this person becomes self-illuminated. There are no chariots, spans, roads. But he projects from himself chariots, spans, roads. There are no blisses there, no pleasures, no delights. But he projects from himself blisses, pleasures, delights. . . . For he is a creator."

The earliest religious texts among the people of the Indus River valley, known as the *Vedas*, included a variety of practical measures to please the gods, including prayers, ethical precepts, and instructions for rituals and sacrifices. At some point after the *Vedas*, another kind of religious text emerged, the *Upanishads*, written by unknown figures over many centuries (Hindu authors traditionally did not attach their names to their writings). Turning the focus of religious practice inward, the *Upanishads* presents a kind of mystical philosophy of the self. The spiritual insights in these texts can be profound, and, in the realm of dream research, highly relevant to our present-day concerns.

The *Brihadaranyaka Upanishad* presents a model of dream formation that seems to rely on nothing other than the creative power of the dreamer's own mind. No gods or demons are involved, no journeys of the soul, no mingling with spirit beings. All that appears in dreaming, according to this text, is projected from the dreamer, drawing on the energy of "his own brightness, his own light." This might sound like a surprisingly modern theory, close to what we dream researchers today call the neurocognitive approach. And yet the *Brihadaranyaka Upanishad* places dreams within a bigger framework of the spiritual evolution of consciousness. The text describes four basic states of being: waking, dreaming, dreamless sleep, and *turiya*, which is a transcendent state of divine immersion and infinite consciousness. In this setting, the exploration of dreaming becomes a valuable source of spiritual growth.

This realization—that the inner light of your unconscious generates the worlds of your dreams—can become a stepping stone toward the higher realization that the divine light creates the world of your waking reality. Just as God creates the universe, you create your dreams. To see more of that creative power in yourself is to see more of it in the world too.

The next three chapters will introduce you to the biggest opportunities—and biggest dangers—in the future of spiritual dreaming. Now that we've looked at the basic dream practices and the most vivid realms of dreaming, we are ready to consider contemporary efforts to use dreams for conscious growth, creative inspiration, and technological enhancement. I hope the previous chapters have given you both a grounding in your own sense of spirit in dreaming and a good critical perspective for the discussions ahead, which highlight a variety of ethical conflicts and questions. We need you and all the other spiritual dreamers of today to get involved in these discussions. The possibilities for insight, healing, and creativity are amazing, but there are also potential problems when people try to manipulate or control dreaming. Finding the right balance of enthusiasm and caution is the goal.

In these final chapters of the book, we will try to do what dreamer-artist and film director David Lynch calls "catching the big fish": diving within ourselves to capture the big ideas that really matter. The insights discussed in the previous chapters are important, and they have helped us arrive at deeper understanding of the spirituality of dreaming. But in the contemporary study of dreams, the biggest of big fish for many researchers is consciousness—specifically the kind of consciousness that appears in *lucid dreams*. Here are a couple of examples collected by pioneering researcher Celia Green in her 1968 book *Lucid Dreams*:

> On pulling up the blind, we made the amazing discovery that the row of houses opposite had vanished and in their place were bare fields. I said to my wife, "This means I am dreaming, though everything seems so real and I feel perfectly awake. Those houses could not disappear in the night, and look at all that grass!" . . .

> Dreaming that I was walking along a road—straight and I think walled on one side—and realized I was dreaming. I knew this was a thing I had been trying to do and thought, "Now I can make something happen." I thought I would like to have an apple. I saw a patch on the road ahead and thought, "By the time I reach

that it will be an apple." Before reaching it, I found I had another apple in my hand. I examined it, thinking, "Quite a creditable imitation of an apple."

Maybe you have experienced dreams like this yourself, in which you were aware of being within a dream. Perhaps you have never had a dream like that, and you are curious why some people get so excited about the idea. In this chapter, we will explore the spiritual appeal and the potential pitfalls of expanded consciousness in dreaming. We will look at references in other historical traditions for teachings about conscious dreams, along with current research on the human mind's powers of *metacognition*, or thinking about thinking. As we shall see, there is a tremendous amount and variety of metacognitive activity in dreaming. Expanding awareness within dreaming is thus an important way of transforming consciousness itself, in both waking and dreaming. This can have tremendous spiritual value in liberating our minds from artificial limits that block our awareness of painful but important truths. It's not something to try on a whim, however. Any practice that seeks to alter the natural unfolding of our dreams can have unintended consequences. The challenge, then, is how to reach a dynamic balance between excitement *and* caution, between promoting conscious growth in dreaming and promoting a healthy respect for the spiritual autonomy of our unconscious minds.

The Lucid Dreaming Debate

For as long as I have been in the field, researchers have been arguing about the nature and significance of lucid dreaming. Several issues consistently elicit strongly opposing points of view. Over the years, I have heard friends and colleagues on both sides of these issues go after each other with great gusto. This debate generates a lot of energy; something important is clearly at stake. Before going any further, let's focus on the key ideas in this discussion about lucidity, or consciousness, in sleep. What follows is an imagined dialogue between an advocate (A) for lucid dreaming and a skeptic (S) of the advocate's claims. Although the phrasing is mine, I can assure you the ideas and sentiments expressed are widely shared on their respective sides.

A: Lucid dreaming is the next stage in the evolution of dreaming.

S: Lucid dreaming may not be real dreaming at all but rather a kind of micro-awakening during REM sleep or at sleep onset.

A: Lucid dreams involve amazing experiences of transcendent power and intensified consciousness.

S: Lucidity actually disrupts dreaming by inserting the waking ego into imaginal processes. The appeal of lucidity while dreaming is the offer of a new and seemingly limitless way of satisfying the ego's desire for control.

A: Lucid dreaming is already showing valuable results as a resource in psychotherapy. People who are chronic nightmare sufferers or trauma victims can learn, through lucid dreaming, to overcome recurrent fears and develop a healthy sense of agency and independence.

S: The emphasis on changing and manipulating dreams in lucid dreaming therapy has a serious downside: obscuring and perhaps diminishing the appearance of healing insights from the unconscious. The emergence of these insights in dreaming depends on the waking ego's temporary withdrawal.

A: Athletes, artists, and innovators of all kinds can use lucid dreaming as a resource for problem-solving and skill-building.

S: These same people could also learn amazing things about their inner creativity if they simply paid more attention to their dreams over time, without trying to manipulate anything. If they just listened for the subtle wisdom of their own unconscious to emerge in their dreams, they wouldn't be so enthralled with the idea of lucid dreaming.

A: Skeptics overlook the historical and cross-cultural fact that experiences of lucid dreaming have been reported all over the world. Contemporary research on lucid dreaming is trying to renew our appreciation for a fundamental power of dreaming that Western rationalists have been trying to dismiss for ages.

S: The practices of lucid dreaming today have much less in common with cross-cultural traditions than the advocates claim. Those non-Western traditions treated consciousness in sleep as part of a bigger system of spiritual practices. People in the modern West are more likely to treat lucid dreaming as a kind of videogame for the indulgence of ego fantasies.

A: Many people today are attracted to lucid dreaming precisely because it opens up new spiritual dimensions of their lives. As they learn more about the potentials for consciousness in dreaming, they learn more about developing greater consciousness in waking life too.

S: It's not mind-expanding; it's dream-limiting and ego-inflating.

A: The most powerfully spiritual lucid dream experiences involve an emphasis on greater *awareness* of what is happening in the dream space, not on trying to *control* it.

S: In the modern West, it's *always* about control.

A: Have *you* ever had a lucid dream?

S: That's irrelevant.

A: No, it's very relevant. If you have never had a lucid dream yourself, how can you really know what you are criticizing? Are you sure you're not just envious of what you hear other people say about the experience?

S: I'm expressing concerns about the misuse of dream research to support scams that lure in gullible people with the promise that, for a price, they can learn how to control and manipulate their dreams. Go ahead and type "lucid dreaming" into an internet search engine; see what comes up.

A: All we can do is teach the best ideas and practices about lucid dreaming. What people do with that information is up to them.

S: A "buyer beware" approach is an awfully low ethical standard for dream research. Some people can become psychologically disturbed by attempting lucid dream practices. Isn't it the responsibility of researchers to acknowledge this to the public and examine the problem more carefully to see what's going on?

A: There is no incompatibility here; researchers on lucid dreaming and on dreaming in general can work together. For example, any growth-oriented approach to dreams can benefit from the enhanced awareness afforded by lucidity.

S: Lucid dreaming is ultimately just a narcissistic parlor trick.

A: Lucid dreaming is the next stage in the evolution of dreaming.

S: Lucid dreaming may not be real dreaming at all . . .

And around and around it goes. The debate about lucid dreaming, if it continues long enough, ends up looping back on itself like an *ouroboros*, the serpent who bites its own tail. That may seem like an image of futility—neither side is right, the debate never ends, the two sides just go around and around—but I believe it reflects an image of paradoxical spiritual wisdom. What if the oppositional dialogue between these two perspectives of truth—the advocate and the skeptic—could be synthesized into something entirely new? Let's see if we can catch a glimpse of what that synthesis might look like—a glimpse, in other words, of the future of consciousness in dreaming.

Cross-Cultural Traditions

Sometimes the future looks remarkably like the past. We in the modern West did not "discover" lucid dreaming. As indicated by the opening quote from the *Upanishads*, people throughout history have been familiar with variations in self-awareness within dreaming. In later Buddhist traditions in India, China, and elsewhere, efforts were made to extend classic practices of meditation into sleep, with the resulting insight into the self-created nature of reality. Here is a passage from *The Life of Milarepa*, a sacred autobiography by a famous Tibetan Buddhist sage from the eleventh century CE:

> During the day I had the sensation of being able to change my body at will and of levitating through space and performing miracles. At night in my dreams I could

freely and without obstacles explore the entire universe from one end to the other. And, transforming myself into hundreds of different material and spiritual bodies, I visited all the Buddha realms and listened to the teachings there. Also, I could preach the Dharma to a multitude of beings. My body could be both in flames and spouting water. Having thus obtained inconceivably miraculous powers, I meditated joyfully and with heightened spirit.

This sounds like a peak lucid dreaming experience. And yet, in the context of Milarepa's life and spiritual development, it only marked a momentary stage in his further growth. Two points are crucial here: first, Milarepa's incredible powers did not appear instantly but only after years of patient training and meditation practice. There is no fast and easy method for having these kinds of dreams. And second, Milarepa did not become attached to these powers, as if becoming a magician was the goal; rather, he let them fall by the wayside as he moved forward in his spiritual journey.

A similar insight comes in another classic work of Asian spirituality, *The Inner Chapters* by the Daoist sage Zhuang Zi in the third century CE. You may already be familiar with this text, in which Zhuang Zi shares an extremely vivid dream of being a butterfly, flying freely in the air. Then he suddenly wakes up and wonders if he's a man who dreamed of being a butterfly or a butterfly who is now dreaming of being a man. What's important isn't that he had an amazing dream of flying—although that's always a wonderful experience. For Zhuang Zi and the Daoist tradition, his dream offers a memorably poetic expression of the higher truth of the transformation of all things. Within this lineage of spiritual wisdom and practice, gaining magical powers matters far less than learning to recognize the endless flow of consciousness as it shifts from one state to another.

These examples make it clear that members of all three major religious traditions of Asia—Hinduism, Buddhism, and Daoism—have been familiar for thousands of years with experiences of self-awareness in dreaming. More than that, all three of these traditions have developed practices aimed at cultivating these kinds of dream experiences and channeling their energies toward spiritual growth and enlightenment.

Much less attention to the conscious dimensions of dreaming appears in Western history. Although the ancient Greek philosopher Aristotle mentions in passing the occurrence of self-awareness in dreaming, he gives no special attention to it. The rise of the Abrahamic traditions of Judaism, Christianity, and Islam put more emphasis on the *content* of dreams as messages of divine reassurance and prophetic warning. But they bracketed out the questions Zhuang Zi and other Asian mystics were asking about the *form* of dreaming as a state of consciousness. The example from Augustine we considered in chapter 6 offers a perfect example. He recounts an instance in which his friend was fully self-aware within the dream, and yet the focus of Augustine's analysis is entirely on the dream's message about the eternal life of the soul and not on what is happening in the mind when someone has a dream like this.

This disinclination in the West to explore self-awareness in dreams increased after the Enlightenment, which drew sharp lines between reason and emotion, reality and illusion, consciousness and the unconscious. A telling example of the Enlightenment attitude toward dreaming comes from eighteenth-century Scottish philosopher Thomas Reid, who wrote a letter to a friend in which he described the recurrent nightmares he suffered as a teenager. The nightmares became so bad that he tried to stop them by force of will, telling himself before bed that dreams aren't real and he wasn't in any danger. The next time a nightmare occurred, he became aware it was a dream and deliberately woke himself out of it. Not only did this end the nightmare; Reid effectively stifled his capacity for dreaming. As one of his biographers writes, "Shortly thereafter Reid stopped remembering any dreams and was subjectively dreamless for almost 40 years."

Eventually, in modern Western society, it no longer became possible, as a matter of linguistic usage and common sense, even to *speak* about self-awareness in dreaming. Talking about being aware, in a dream, that you were dreaming was like talking about the coolness of fire or the softness of a rock: you were just contradicting yourself and making no sense.

Of course, ideological language games like this have not completely stopped people from experiencing dreams with dramatic variations in consciousness; scattered examples can be found through the centuries. But the combined arguments from theological and philosophical authorities did succeed in excluding the topic from respectable circles of Western intellectual discussion until the latter part of the twentieth century. People could still talk about lucid dreams in the context of occult and esoteric writings, but these reports were often meandering and impressionistic, making it easy for mainstream scientists to dismiss them out of hand.

Making broad generalizations about something as complex and multifaceted as human religiosity is difficult. Yet the historical evidence suggests a real difference of attitude toward lucid dreaming between the Asian religious traditions of Hinduism,

Buddhism, and Daoism, on the one hand, and the Abrahamic traditions of Judaism, Christianity, and Islam, on the other. Most Indigenous cultures, especially those with shamanic practices, would side with the Asian religious traditions on this issue. The former group, by and large, acknowledges the varieties of consciousness in dreams and sees this as a spiritual opportunity. The latter group, by and large, ignores consciousness in dreaming and regards it as spiritually irrelevant. Once again, no judgment is implied in one direction or the other. Neither perspective is automatically right or wrong. If nothing else, this historical background suggests that the current excitement about lucid dreaming in the modern West might represent a kind of cultural rebound effect. Perhaps many of us are experiencing a new surge of interest in lucid dreaming because our culture has paid such minimal attention to this aspect of our dreaming selves for centuries.

Thinking about Thinking

Let's step back for a moment and consider more carefully what we mean when we're talking about consciousness in dreaming. In an early study of lucid dreaming, psychologist Sheila Purcell and her colleagues at University of Ottawa developed a "self-reflectiveness scale" as a way of highlighting variations in how the mind works during a dream. Here is my slightly elaborated version of their nine-point scale of dreaming, which they categorize in terms of the "process level" of dreaming.

1. *A truck drives down a street.* (The dreamer isn't in the dream; there are no other people, just unfamiliar objects.)
2. *My cat climbs on the sofa.* (The dreamer isn't in the dream, but it has familiar characters, objects, and settings.)

3. *I am running on a beach, trying to catch up to my friends.*
   (The dreamer is completely immersed in the drama of
   the dream, with a first-person perspective.)
4. *I'm at a store, watching as the manager and a customer argue
   about something.* (The dreamer is present but primarily as
   an observer of the action.)
5. *I tell them I have a better idea how to use their leftover
   food.* (The dreamer thinks something over and/or com-
   municates with another character.)
6. *Suddenly I was the waiter, taking other people's drink orders.*
   (The dreamer is transformed in some way, prompting a
   new perspective.)
7. *I was driving the car but also watching from outside, and I
   saw the car was a weird color.* (The dreamer has multiple
   perspectives, participating and observing and/or noticing
   anomalies.)
8. *I lead a group of people in building a circular structure in
   the jungle, but when a jaguar leaps at me, I get scared and
   wake myself up.* (The dreamer has a high degree of agency
   within the dream and can wake up deliberately.)
9. *I see the pages in the book look strange, and I realize I must
   be dreaming.* (The dreamer can consciously reflect on
   being within a dream.)

Does this help you see the different ways the mind processes
our experiences in dreaming? Dreams being dreams, there will
always be instances with overlapping categories and instances
that don't fit into any category. But this framework can give
you a new way of reflecting on your own dreams and how you
are mentally processing your experiences while dreaming. You
may also want to think of particular dreams you've experienced
that had unusual variations of self-awareness from your usual

processing mode and consider which new perspectives may be opening up for you.

In a survey Purcell and her colleagues conducted among a large population of college students, the dreams they analyzed most often fell into categories 5, 3, and 7 (in that order). This fits pretty well with my own experiences as well. Dreams of thinking and speaking (5), being completely immersed in a dreaming action (3), and multiple perspectives while noticing oddities (7): these are very familiar, and the dreams in each category clearly involve the activation of a distinctive suite of cognitive functions and thus a distinctive mode of dreaming consciousness. One of the values of this approach is that it shows how the metacognitive powers of the mind are highly active in many kinds of dreams, not just those at the far end of the scale (8, 9). In addition to surveys, Purcell and her colleagues also experimented with simple methods to stimulate lucid dreaming, and they found that many of their participants responded positively to these methods. This led them to the remarkable conclusion that the capacity for lucid dreaming can be limited by the mental framework of the dreamer and *not* by the innate potentials of dreaming itself. If someone consciously denies the possibility of self-awareness in dreaming, then that belief will likely inhibit their experiences in that realm. But that's a self-fulfilling prophecy that cannot serve as scientific evidence. In other words, just because you don't have (or don't *want* to have) a certain kind of dream doesn't mean those dreams don't exist at all and that no one else experiences them.

Purcell and her coauthors emphasize that these psychological limits and constraints are not fixed. They can change. Simply by paying more attention to your dreams and making room for them in your waking mind, the constraints begin to lift, and new possibilities of dreaming consciousness can emerge.

Cultures of Control

Many people who study dreams are wary of the topic of lucid dreaming for one big reason: Jung said virtually nothing about it. Neither, it is true, did Freud. But it's Jung's silence that hangs heaviest over contemporary dream research. If lucid dreaming is such a profound source of psychological and spiritual value, why didn't Jung ever mention it?

Jung describes many of his own dreams and the dreams of his patients, and he writes at length about the nature of dreaming and the many different forms it takes. Yet he never shows any special interest in the possibility that one could become conscious within the dream and control its contents. On the contrary, the core tenets of his psychology leave little room for the ego-forward lucid dreaming practices of many contemporary advocates.

Consider this passage, the gist of which could be found in any number of Jung's other writings: "Dreams are impartial, spontaneous products of the unconscious psyche, outside the control of the will. They are pure nature; they show us the unvarnished, natural truth, and are therefore fitted, as nothing else is, to give us back an attitude that accords with our basic human nature when our consciousness has strayed too far from its foundations and run into an impasse." From a Jungian perspective, it is precisely the *unconscious* aspects of dreaming that make it so valuable for psychological and spiritual growth. In dreams, we connect with something bigger than our waking selves. The energies of our inner nature come to the fore, disclosing fundamental truths with direct personal relevance. From what we might call a hard Jungian viewpoint, the desire to "go lucid" in one's dreams is itself a sign of psychological imbalance and unhealthy ego attachments.

And yet . . . when we look at the latest findings of the neuroscience of consciousness, it's almost impossible not to feel
intensely curious about the amazing range and variety of possibilities of self-awareness in dreaming. The desire to explore those
possibilities and learn more about them seems like something we
should encourage, not criticize. A Jungian perspective can seem
stuffy and overly conservative in its insistence that we do nothing but passively receive whatever comes in our dreams. What's
so wrong with becoming more actively engaged with the deeper
processes of dreaming?

At the least—and this is the strongest argument of lucid
dreaming advocates—the capacity for greater *awareness* in
dreaming enables people to learn more about their dreams.
Lucid dreaming has obvious benefits for a psychology like
Jung's, where practices to stimulate greater self-awareness in
dreaming could help patients make greater progress in identifying archetypal symbols and unconscious complexes. Lucid
awareness, not lucid control, can respect the dreaming process
while increasing its beneficial impact on the waking mind. This
approach sounds reasonable and conciliatory, and it gestures
in the right direction, but it is still problematic if it does not
account for the social circumstances in which people today are
learning about lucid dreaming. Simply put: *culture matters*, in
dreaming as in other aspects of our lives. The culture of the
modern West strongly emphasizes the values of consumerism,
control, speed, power, and personal pleasure. In that cultural
context, it should not be surprising if people are inclined to use
lucid dreaming in the service of those values. It doesn't *have* to
be this way; culture doesn't determine everything. But more
often than advocates of lucid dreaming seem willing to recognize, the "awareness, not control" message is drowned out by a

much louder chorus of cultural voices saying, "Control whatever you can; it's fun!"

Much of the energy around lucid dreaming right now comes from the gaming industry, where the experience of playing an immersive videogame is often described as having a "dreamlike" quality. The gold standard for many game developers is exactly this: to create something that feels as real and all-embracing and stimulating as an actual dream. For the hundreds of millions of people deeply involved in these games—no one should underestimate the size and enthusiasm of the gaming community—it makes intuitive sense that lucid dreaming could be developed into a kind of personalized videogame. *And* it makes sense that professional developers are actively working to make their games, virtual reality adventures, and metaverse scenarios as thoroughly dreamlike as possible.

Here we find a kind of double-cultural metaphor: lucid dreaming becomes a model for videogames, and videogames become a model for lucid dreaming. I have no problem with the first part of the metaphor but lots of problems with the second. To think of dreaming as analogous to a gaming experience requires a drastic narrowing of the oneiric imagination. Dreams are not technologically mediated fantasies built out of zeroes and ones, mass produced as commodities for commercial and entertainment purposes. Dreams emerge from an embodied, genetically rooted process, one that is intimately interwoven with the whole span of the individual's existence. They bring forth unconscious images and energies of utter novelty and originality, with direct relevance to a dreamer's waking-life concerns.

Dreams, lucid or otherwise, have many more differences than similarities to videogames. And yet we already have research findings that point to a strong positive connection between frequency of videogame playing and frequency of lucid dreaming. If, as seems almost certain, the experience of gaming influences the patterns of people's dreams, it may diminish the emergence of "unknown unknowns" in dreaming: the startlingly unexpected insights that seem to come out of nowhere. Those insights come from outside the sphere of my conscious ego or anyone else's conscious ego. A videogame model of dreaming obscures this subtle but vital truth. How can we know we're missing something if we don't acknowledge it was there in the first place?

"Speak, for Thy Servant Hears"

A story from the Bible sheds light on this debate about lucid dreaming in surprisingly helpful ways. The story comes from the first book of Samuel, at the very beginning of his prophetic career. Samuel was a twelve-year-old boy helping the elderly, nearly blind Eli with his responsibilities for caring for the Temple that held the ark of the covenant, the holiest of all objects to the Jewish people. One night, Eli was sleeping outside the Temple, while Samuel "was lying down within the temple of the Lord where the ark of God was." God called out to Samuel twice by name, and Samuel arose and went outside to Eli. "Here I am, for you called me," he said. Eli replied, "I did not call; lie down again." So Samuel went back inside and lay down.

The Lord called his name again; Samuel arose and went outside to Eli, who said it was not him: "I did not call, my son; lie down again." Samuel returned to the Temple and lay down, and then a third time the Lord called. When Samuel came outside again, Eli realized what was happening: "Therefore Eli said to Samuel, 'Go, lie down; and if he calls you, you shall say, "Speak, Lord, for thy servant hears."'"

So Samuel returned to the Temple, and when "the Lord came and stood forth, calling as at other times," he replied just as Eli instructed. God then proclaimed, "Behold, I am about to do a thing in Israel, at which the two ears of every one that hears it will tingle." After listening to God's terrible prophecy that a brutal war was coming, "Samuel lay until morning; then he opened the doors of the house of the Lord." (See 1 Samuel 3 for the whole story.) Although reluctant to be the bearer of bad news, Samuel shared the dream revelation with Eli.

To make sense of this story, it helps to know some cultural and theological background. Samuel likely lived in the seventh or eighth century BCE, when Judaism was one small religious tradition among many other larger civilizations in ancient Mesopotamia, including the Babylonians, Akkadians, and Egyptians. In those other traditions, dreaming was considered a primary means of communication between humans and the gods. Judaism agreed with them about the religious value of dreams, but with one important difference: the Jews put much less emphasis on the practice of dream incubation. For all the other Mesopotamian religions, dream incubation was a regular method for eliciting divine revelations about any number of different topics. By contrast, the God of Judaism did not respond to a summons like a dream incubation ritual. The majesty and grandeur of the Lord was so great that humans could never expect, let alone produce, a dream revelation.

This context has two implications for understanding the story of Samuel. First, the location where he lay down for the night represents, from a Mesopotamian perspective, a perfect place to perform a dream incubation ritual. As we discussed earlier, when people seek to incubate a dream, they usually go away from their normal, ordinary world and toward a place of spiritual power: a mountain, cave, graveyard, or, as in this case, a temple. Here, we do not have just any temple, but *the* Temple, the central house of Jewish worship, which housed the ark of the covenant itself. For a Jew, there simply could not be a more religiously charged place to sleep. The story provides the perfect setup for a classic Mesopotamian dream incubation ritual intended to produce a divine revelation.

And this is indeed how it turns out—but not until Samuel has failed three times to heed the Lord's call. Why is Samuel so slow to understand what's actually happening? Because as a faithful Jew, he does not expect God to make a personal appearance in his dreams, no matter where he was sleeping. This is the second implication of the story's theological context. The ancient Jews tried to distinguish their faith from the others around them by elevating the majesty and autonomy of Yahweh, unlike the more servile deities of other Mesopotamian cultures. This meant less interest in dream incubation rituals in Judaism, a point that is dramatized in this story. Samuel was such a good, virtuous, and God-fearing youth that he could lie down at night inside the Temple right next to the ark of the covenant, hear a voice calling his name again and again, and *not* assume it was God reaching out to him. Any other Mesopotamian person at that time would immediately know what was happening. But not Samuel! His obliviousness is the point—it's behavioral proof of his deep humility and respect for the Lord.

Eventually Eli set him straight, and Samuel reentered the Temple, ready now to respond properly if and when the Lord called him again: "Speak, for thy servant hears." This, I suggest, can be understood as a parable about lucid dreaming. Samuel's story has many other meanings, of course, but I believe it neatly encapsulates the lucid dreaming debate and provides a model for a spiritually balanced approach to self-awareness in dreams. The Babylonians, Assyrians, Egyptians, and other ancient Mesopotamian peoples took a more active approach to the potential for religious experiences in dreaming, while the Jewish people considered that a form of spiritual arrogance that disrespected God's autonomous power and wisdom. And yet Samuel found a way, with blind old Eli's guidance, to do both. He found a way to honor God's supreme independence *and* to carry out the personal intention to remain present, self-aware, and highly attentive during the revelatory experience.

Here we can see the outlines of an approach that, shifted from theology to dream research, can do justice to both sides of the lucid dreaming debate. As a matter of spiritual practice, efforts to enhance your consciousness in dreaming can be beneficial—if you can truly suspend your ego attachments. That's a very big *if*, however. This is why Buddhism, Hinduism, and other religious traditions require people to undergo years of training and guidance to prepare them for lucid dream experiences. The ultimate challenge here is how to ground your explorations of lucid dreaming within your spiritual or religious worldview, whatever that may be. This is worth pondering before you begin experimenting with changes to the dynamics of your sleeping mind. If you really want to experience lucid dreaming, the best, most effective thing you can do is first answer a simple question: *why?*

CHAPTER 8

Play
Dreaming to Create Reality

For many people who study dreams, the big fish they seek isn't just enhanced consciousness, it's greater creative power. They look to dreams as a valuable resource for artists, innovators, activists, and anyone trying to solve problems and think outside the box. By cultivating dreaming, we cultivate the deepest powers of our imagination, ultimately connecting us with the beating heart of our spiritual nature. Dreams have truly infinite creativity at their disposal. They can put us in any place, with anyone, doing anything. This open-ended dynamism emerges from the very core of the dreaming imagination. It is the birthright of all humans; we are all fundamentally creative beings.

D. W. Winnicott, a British psychoanalyst, was one of the first to see the vital connection among dreams, play, creativity, and culture. In his 1970 book *Playing and Reality*, he said, "In playing, the child manipulates external phenomena in service of the dream and invests chosen external phenomena with dream meaning and feeling." Winnicott continued, "There is a direct development from transitional phenomena to playing, and from playing to shared playing, and from this to cultural experiences." This chapter will explore the many impressive ways in which dreaming contributes to artistic creativity in fields like literature, music, and film. The dream-play-art relationship has spiritual dimensions, both for the creators and their audiences, which we will discuss too. To start, I'll share my ideas about dreaming as a kind of *play*: the play of the imagination during sleep.

Dreaming Is Play

You might be surprised at how many dream researchers believe that dreaming has no real function. They grant that dreams can be meaningful and interesting to study insofar as they reflect the important concerns of our waking life. But these researchers do not see any essential *purpose* for dreaming. People's use of their dreams in waking life does not mean the dreams themselves are intrinsically functional in any way. Just because you can make a flute out of a piece of wood doesn't mean the function of trees is to produce musical instruments.

Several answers may have leaped to your mind in response to this claim that dreaming has no psychological function. Before you go too far, though, consider what's involved in a theory of dream function. It needs to account for all dreams from all people. And not just all remembered dreams but dreaming *as such*, regardless of the vagaries of recall. The theory needs to account for the multiplicity of dreams, for all the various types of dreaming experiences, from the littlest to the biggest. It needs to show how dreaming is grounded in the nature of sleep and the evolved structures of the brain and how it contributes to our biological survival. And it should explain the cultural connections found in human communities all over the world linking dreams, dream-sharing, creativity, and art.

This is a tall order! But it is not an impossible set of standards to achieve. I have argued elsewhere that the idea of *dreaming as a kind of play* meets all of these standards. Here, I would simply like to persuade you that thinking of dreaming as play will shed new light on the creative dynamics of art and spirituality—and perhaps even the emergence of culture itself.

I am not the first researcher to notice the connection between dreaming and play. Among the earliest were psychologists who worked with children. Studies by Jean Piaget, Erik Erikson, and D. W. Winnicott, among others, showed that ordinary children's play is actually a psychologically rich mode of imaginal behavior with many of the same qualities we find in dreaming: spontaneity, wide variability, deep immersion, and open-endedness. I knew something about these ideas not just from the classroom (my doctoral program focused heavily on developmental psychology) but also from my part-time work during graduate school as an afternoon teacher at an elementary school. My job was fairly simple because the regular school day was over, and now the kids were free to do nothing but play. I had plenty of time to observe their play and think about it in relation to the dynamics of dreaming. To an outside observer, children's play might look like purely random activities, with no meaning or purpose whatsoever. Yet researchers in child development have shown quite clearly that play is a vital activity in the growth and maturation not only of humans but also of nearly all mammalian species and many birds too. I saw a clear parallel with dreams, which also seem "bizarre" and nonsensical from an outside perspective and yet have tremendous structure and meaning once you know what to look for.

The question then became: does this apparent similarity lead to any deeper insight about the function of either play or dreaming? Researchers who study play in humans and other animal species emphasize the following features of play as important for understanding its functional value:

1. Play actions are partial and incomplete compared to their serious counterparts; for example, a play fight does not go as far as a real fight.
2. Play is spontaneous, pleasurable, rewarding, and/or voluntary; it feels fun, although sometimes it can become so intense and immersive that negative emotions arise too.
3. Play is different from serious behaviors in form and in timing. Play is always most prominent in the youngest members of a species.
4. Play involves behaviors that are repeated but with variations.
5. Play emerges in the absence of severe stress; it depends on some degree of freedom from the ordinary demands of life.

For a behavior to have so many recurrent features across nearly all mammalian and avian species, its function must have very deep evolutionary roots. Although several questions remain, a picture has emerged indicating that the basic function of play is to *prepare* a creature, especially in its youth, for the survival-related activities that will be the primary business of its adult life. These activities include seeking prey and avoiding predators, procreating, exploring, and grooming. Play provides a safe space in which to practice new and different behaviors, to prepare for the dangers and opportunities of the future, to rehearse possible responses, and to envision alternative scenarios.

Particularly for social species in which interpersonal relations occupy much of life, play becomes an important arena for developing the diplomatic skills necessary for survival. A great deal of research has been done on the play behaviors of non-human primates like chimpanzees, bonobos, and gorillas. The functional value of group play is very clear in helping these species navigate complex social networks, not only in youth but also in adulthood.

When I talk about dreaming as play, I am not speaking metaphorically. Dreaming is not merely like play or analogous to play. It *is* play: dreaming is the imaginative play that occurs within the conditions of sleep. Dreams can be characterized by all the features that researchers have found in cross-species play behaviors: they are only partially realistic; they are spontaneous and bizarre, with recurrent features of content; and they can be disrupted by stress. Dreaming and play share a strong kinship of psychological form and evolutionary development. Indeed, dreaming may represent a kind of "pure play," in which perceptions from external reality are bracketed out to a maximal degree, allowing the imagination total freedom to simulate worlds of immersive experience with horizons of endless possibility.

Now that you know I think about dreams in this way, you'll see the overarching theme in most of the points I have been making in this book. What's the best way to interpret dreams? *Play with them.* What's the best way to share dreams? *Play with them, with others.* How should you deal with the disruptive unconscious energies embodied in the archetype of the shadow? *Play with them.* How can you bring the healing effects of pre-death dreams and visions into the waking world? *Play with them.* What is the most spiritually responsible way to explore lucid dreams? *Play with them.* Now you can also see the basis on which

I shower praise in some directions and cast aspersions in others. It's all about play. If a theory, belief, or practice enhances our appreciation for the intrinsic playfulness of dreaming, I will usually support it. If, however, a theory, belief, or practice diminishes or discourages our recognition of the playful dynamics of dreaming, I will usually criticize it.

And now you can perhaps see, from a new angle, why I defined spirituality the way I did in the introduction: by emphasizing the sense of dynamic movement, vitality, and transformation. These qualities all characterize the most powerful forms of play. In a way, spirituality is a living sense of *cosmic play*: the play of creation itself and our intimate involvement in it. Living a life of spirit means participating fully in this playful, continually unfolding process of self-revelation and self-transcendence.

To illustrate what these ideas and concepts look like in practice (thanks again, John McDargh!), let's consider some of the well-documented instances of artists' dreams, that is, dreams that had a significant impact on a prominent work of art. Scientific researchers generally do not regard such accounts as legitimate evidence, treating them as unverifiable anecdotes. Of course, individual reports of unusual dreams are indeed liable to distortions of various kinds, so we need to be careful. But a single, focused case study can also legitimately reveal new processes that later experiments confirm in a broader population. What follows are several individual cases of artistically influential dreams that, considered as a whole, reveal the dynamic relationship between dreaming and creativity.

Literature

We have already mentioned how Robert Louis Stevenson, the Scottish novelist, drew his idea for the plot of the *Strange Case of*

Dr. Jekyll and Mr. Hyde from a dream in which he gained insight into humanity's inherent doubleness. Stevenson attributed many of his stories to the nocturnal activities of what he called "the Little People": impish supernatural beings like the Brownies of Scottish highlands folklore. He realized this phenomenon had bigger implications for understanding the nature of human creativity: "The more I think of it, the more I am moved to press upon the world my question: Who are the Little People? They are near connections of the dreamer's beyond doubt," he wrote. "They have plainly learned like him to build the scheme of a considerable story in progressive order; only I think they have more talent; and one thing is beyond doubt, they can tell him a story piece by piece, like a serial, and keep him all the while in ignorance of where they aim. Who are they, then? And who is the dreamer?"

A more poignant example involves the English novelist Mary Godwin Shelley, who in 1815 gave birth prematurely to a baby girl, who died just a few days later. Mary, who was seventeen at the time, fell into a deep depression. About a month after the baby's death, she had the following dream (March 19), which she recorded in her journal: "Dreamt that my little baby came to life again; that it had only been cold, and that we rubbed it before the fire, and it lived. Awake and find no baby. I think about the little thing all day. Not in good spirits."

Shelley's long process of mourning, punctuated by this sorrowful dream, became an unexpected source of creative inspiration. Within a year, she had birthed another child, a son who survived, and the following summer she and her eventual husband, the poet Percy Shelley, visited Lord Byron at his Swiss estate on the shores of Lake Geneva. Byron was one of the great literary figures of the age, and to amuse themselves while together, the three of them engaged in a contest of competitive storytelling to see who could devise the most frightening story of the maca-bre and the supernatural. Mary's tale, about a mad scientist who stitches corpses together and brings the resulting creature to life, won the prize, and it became the seed for her first novel: *Frankenstein, or, The Modern Prometheus*. The novel reflects the same bring-the-dead-back-to-life fantasy as in her dream but with significant differences: Mary's dream involves a mother trying to revive her naturally born child, while the story has a male scientist fabricating an unnatural monster. In *Frankenstein*, Mary adds to her dream a dimension of uncanny horror, along with a prescient critique of the masculine grandiosity and self-destructive hubris of modern science.

The novelist and short story writer Franz Kafka, originally from Bohemia in what is now the Czech Republic, suffered from disturbed sleep and lifelong nightmares. He mentioned several specific dreams in his diaries and letters, which the psychologist Calvin Hall and a colleague gathered and analyzed. They found several recurrent themes in Kafka's dreams: bodily preoccupa-tions, concerns about physical disfigurement, and clothing and personal appearance. These themes also predominated in Kafka's waking life as he was frequently ill and anxious about his body and appearance; he would ultimately die young of tuberculo-sis. The same themes also characterized much of his fiction—for example, in his novels *The Trial* and *The Castle*, which have the stifling atmosphere of a waking nightmare. This is especially true in his novella *Metamorphosis*, which includes perhaps the worst carryover effect in the history of dreaming. Here are the chilling first lines of the story:

When Gregor Samsa woke up one morning from unset-tling dreams, he found himself changed in bed into a monstrous vermin. He was lying on his back as hard as armor plate, and when he lifted his head a little, he saw his vaulted brown belly, sectioned by arch-shaped ribs, to whose dome the cover, about to slide off completely, could barely cling. His many legs, pitifully thin compared with the size of the rest of him, were waving helplessly before his eyes. "What's happened to me?" he thought. It was no dream.

Kafka's stories express the age-old anxiety that the most monstrous impulses of the unconscious, long contained by traditional moral beliefs, are now breaking through into waking reality.

An excellent resource in the study of dreams and literature is Naomi Epel's *Writers Dreaming*, a collection of interviews with more than two dozen contemporary authors. Among the writers Epel interviews is the poet and memoirist Maya Angelou, who shared a recurrent dream that she felt was a creative ally in her work:

> There is a dream which I delight in and long for when I'm writing. It means to me that the work is going well. Or will go well. Or that I'm telling the truth and telling it well. I dream of a very tall building. It's in the process of being built and there are scaffolds and steps. It looks sort of like the inside of the Arc de Triomphe. I'm climbing it with alacrity and joy and laughter. Quite often it's day but it's not very bright because I'm inside the structure going up. I have no sense of dizziness or discomfort or vertigo. I'm just climbing. I can't tell you how delicious that is! . . . Whenever I get that dream I know the work is going to be all right for about two or three weeks. So that delights my heart.

Angelou also described her writing process as a journey where she goes to "a place that's a little like dreaming. Almost dreaming, but I'm awake. It's an enchantment." Even though she lived in a large house, she kept a room at a nearby hotel, where she went early each morning. Everything had been taken off the walls, and all distracting objects had been removed. On the bed she placed a dictionary, a thesaurus, the Bible, and a deck of playing cards. For a typical book, she would go through two or three decks of cards, playing endless games of solitaire to occupy what she called her "small mind," while the bigger forces of her imagination were free to envision the writing ahead. She commented, "I don't really get down, I don't play the cards. I'm playing at playing. But that's fine. I don't know how this is like dreaming but it is."

Music

A good friend of mine, Nancy Grace, who is both a dream researcher and a talented musician, has written about the dynamics of dream-inspired creativity in the lives of professional musicians from a wide variety of genres. One of the people she profiles is Sting, the singer and bassist who, after a long and successful career leading the rock band The Police, set off on his own musical journey. He was anxious about the making of his first solo album, which he knew would lead in directions his fans might not immediately appreciate.

During this time, he received a surprising image of reassurance from his nocturnal imagination:

I had a dream that I was back home in Hampshire, looking out the window into this big walled-in garden I have out back with its very neat flowerbed and foliage. Suddenly, out of a hole in the wall came these large, macho, aggressive, and quite drunk blue turtles. They started doing backflips and other acrobatics, in the process utterly destroying my garden. . . . I'm enjoying this curious spectacle, and the dream is so strong I remembered it perfectly when I woke up, to the point where it became part of my juggernaut to complete this record. . . . For me, the turtles are symbols of the subconscious, living under the sea, full of unrealized potential, very Jungian in their meaning. . . . So with the album I wanted to destroy a lot of preconceptions and expectations, and do something unsettlingly different. These blue turtles, these musicians, were gonna help me. And they did.

Grace emphasizes that dream-inspired musicians like Sting play an important and yet underappreciated role in promoting dream awareness among the general public. Musicians serve as unofficial ambassadors to the dreaming unconscious, and the enjoyment listeners get from their music becomes a subtle means of learning about the creative power of dreaming. Even more than with albums, streaming, and radio play, the true magic of music emerges in live performance, and Grace makes the vital point that concerts can become spontaneous venues of collective dream-sharing. "A more specific reason that live performances bring the energy of dreams into the community is that during many live musical performances, dreams are being told," she writes. "Given that the oral tradition of community dream-sharing, so common in many traditional cultures, is virtually non-existent in the modern Western world, the concert hall may be one of the few established social venues where dreams are still spoken about freely, regularly, and with enthusiasm."

Film

The contemporary art form most associated with our visions of the night, movies have a rich and varied history of interaction with the study of dreams. The cinematic products of the Dream Factory have been grounded in actual dreaming experience from the earliest days of the medium. Some of the most popular movies in history (e.g., *The Wizard of Oz, The Matrix, Inception*) make dreaming itself the theme of the story. My friend Bernard Welt—he who told me to run in the dream I recounted in chapter 2—has argued that many of the standard conventions of filmmaking derive from typical features of people's dreams. "Basic conventions of narrative cinema reproduce key features of the dream experience, rather than perceptions of external reality as is often assumed," he writes. "For example, the montage technique of cutting from scene to scene with minimal transition, or the symbolic use of spatial relations to convey emotions, are elements of cinema that appear to derive from our dreams, even when they are employed in the service of realism."

In this view, *every* film is a dream film. Every narrative film, whatever the genre and however realistic it appears, operates according to a logic of dreaming. We understand and enjoy the language of cinema because it is the language of our own dreams, projected outward and reflected back to us from the silver screen. High on the list of Bernard's all-time favorite dream movies is the semi-animated *Waking Life* (2003) by US director Richard Linklater. *Waking Life* is a beautiful cinematic exploration of dreaming, consciousness, identity, and transcendence. The medium and the message merge in a uniquely creative way, to the point where the audience doesn't simply become "immersed" in the film so much as existentially implicated in the same web of paradoxes that enchant, amuse, and perplex the characters in the film. Bernard describes the highlights of the movie in these terms:

> Its central character experiences a slowly unfolding set of nested dreams, drifting in and out of a lucid state, moving among other dreamers; increasingly concerned about the possibility that he will never return from the illusions of dreaming to the world of waking. Linklater intensifies the dream atmosphere by using the dream-making capacities of animation (through a rotoscoping process that transforms live-action film sequences into drawings), and frequently trains the audience's attention on the dream-film parallel—encouraging them to experience an unusual lucid film spectatorship, as it were.

In addition to literature, music, and film, we could look at examples from many other forms of art—such as theater, painting, graphic arts, and dance—where dreaming plays a role in stimulating creative innovations. But has the thought crossed your mind that maybe some of these stories are too good to be true? That maybe some of them were fabricated or at least embellished somewhat because the idea of a story, song, or movie coming from a dream makes it seem cooler? It's okay to ask the question; healthy skepticism is a virtue in the study of dreams. The temptation to make up self-aggrandizing dreams has probably been stronger than some artists could resist. But can we reasonably conclude that *all* of these stories are fabricated? That would be quite an extreme form of skepticism and unwarranted by the actual evidence.

We can identify several recurrent themes in the reports just considered that reflect bigger patterns in creative dreaming, patterns that apply across all the variations and possible limitations in each of the individual cases. To begin, we can note that the same creative dynamics of dreaming emerge in three very different artistic media. Writing fiction, playing music, and making a film draw upon widely divergent mental faculties and artistic talents, and yet dreaming directly and powerfully contributes to the creative process for each of them.

We can also observe the frequency with which a dream will provide specific content that the artist incorporates into a work with little or no additional editing. Apparently, the ratio of inspiration to perspiration can vary dramatically depending on the artist and the given project. At the same time, the creative impact of dreaming extends beyond generating new content. Dreams can give an artist an overall sense of aesthetic guidance and encouragement, like Sting's blue turtles and Maya Angelou's exuberant climbing of the tall building. Creatively stimulating dreams can occur spontaneously, apropos of nothing, a pure gift from the unconscious. And yet these dreams also occur in very specific moments of anxiety and crisis in the artists' lives, responding directly to their immediate creative concerns. As Robert Louis Stevenson observed, the creative forces of dreaming are "near connections of the dreamer," attuned to the artist's most intimate personal concerns and yet drawing on chthonic energies from unfathomable realms of the mind.

The most consistent theme in these dreams, I believe, is their playfulness and their extension of the play of dreaming into the play of cultural creativity. Seen in light of the dreaming-is-play theory, the prominence of dreaming among artists is exactly what we would expect. People who devote their waking lives to creative pursuits will almost inevitably stimulate their dreaming imaginations, too, which can generate a positive feedback loop of dreaming at night and waking creativity in the day. Art thus appears as a natural outgrowth of the free play of dreaming and the culmination of a dream's journey from individual sleep to cultural expression and spiritual experience.

One example mentioned above seems completely contrary to the idea of dreaming as play—Mary Godwin Shelley's heartbreaking nightmare of her dead baby coming back to life. How could such a dream possibly be characterized as playful? Rather than helping her face reality, the dream seems like a cruel delusion that taunts her with an image of her child alive again, only to cast her back into the cold waking world, where she must confront the horrible truth anew.

This is a good place to acknowledge that both dreaming and play are fragile. Recall the definition of *play* above, which included "absence of stress" as a condition for the emergence of play. If the stress-inducing threats and dangers of waking life reach a certain threshold of intensity, it becomes difficult and perhaps impossible to dream or to play. This can be seen most vividly in cases of post-traumatic stress disorder (PTSD), one common symptom of which is recurrent nightmares that graphically replay the traumatizing event over and over again. It seems the person's mind does not know how to process the event; the repetitive images and feelings reflect a deep disruption of core feelings of trust and safety in the world and a desperate struggle to integrate the trauma somehow into the person's ongoing sense of self. In that context, we can immediately appreciate the traumatizing effects on Mary of her daughter's death and see some of the classic features of a PTSD nightmare in her dream.

Researchers and therapists today, who have far more experience with traumatized populations than anyone would like, look carefully at the dreams of people with PTSD, seeking signs that the grip of the fixed, graphic repetitions of the trauma might eventually loosen. Healing from PTSD seems to correspond to a change in dreaming: the nightmares gradually diminish in intensity and rigidness, and a more fluid spirit emerges that brings new dynamics into the person's nocturnal imagination. In a word, the dreams become more *playful*. A PTSD nightmare is the antithesis of play. The experience of trauma can have the effect of blocking the naturally playful flow of dreaming. Fortunately, many people can, with enough time and support, recover from a severe trauma to some extent at least. A resumption of normal, healthy, playful dreaming can be a leading indicator of this process.

Only the one dream of Mary's remains from her time of intense mourning, so we do not know if this development occurred in her dreaming. But we do have her astonishing creative work in *Frankenstein*, which I believe can be appreciated as an artistic dream of healing—a transformation of personal suffering and loss into a world-changing creative vision. No longer trapped within her own private sorrow, Mary found a way through her art to channel her painful emotional energies toward a public expression of darkly beautiful collective truth.

CHAPTER 9

Tech

Dreaming to Connect the World

On the run from his enraged older brother Esau, Jacob has fled into the wilderness. "Jacob left Beer-sheba, and went toward Haran," the writer of Genesis tells us. "And he came to a certain place, and stayed there that night, because the sun had set. Taking one of the stones of the place, he put it under his head and lay down in that place to sleep" (Gen 28:10–11). He stops for no other reason than night has fallen and he can travel no farther for now. With equal casualness, he picks up a rock and places it under his head as he lies down to sleep. All the emphasis of the story thus far has been on the urgency of Jacob's desperate escape from Esau and his dangerous solo journey to reach a nearby town, where his mother's relatives will protect him. The nameless location where he happens to be sleeping along the way seems irrelevant to the anxious concerns of his waking life. Yet this brief passage sets up the physical location for Jacob's numinous dream, one of the greatest dream theophanies in the history of religions: of a ladder spanning heaven and earth, with angels ascending and descending upon it. When Jacob awakes from the dream, he has a completely different appreciation for where he has been sleeping. His first words are "'Surely the Lord is in this place—and I did not know it!' And he was afraid and said, 'How awesome is this place! This is none other than the house of God, and this is the gate of heaven'" (Gen 28:16–17).

As it happened to Samuel in the story we discussed in chapter 7, Jacob experienced an unintentional dream incubation. He didn't *mean* to perform a presleep ritual to elicit a revelatory dream; it just worked out that way. In Samuel's case, he slept in the Temple, the spiritual epicenter of his community. Jacob, by contrast, fled as far as he could from his community, and he slept in what seemed to be a completely innocuous, spiritually insignificant place. More than Samuel, he could be forgiven for not expecting a dream revelation in these circumstances.

Yet it turns out that even an obscure spot in the wilderness can have divinely dream-stimulating effects if the conditions are right. The stone that Jacob used as a kind of pillow might seem like a trivial detail, but it actually amplifies the spiritual message of the dream itself. People in the ancient cultures of Africa, Mesopotamia, China, and elsewhere used a variety of solid objects (wood, ceramic, stone) as head or neck rests to aid in their sleep. Although this seems strange and uncomfortable according to our standards for fluffy pillows today, it would not have struck people of that time as an unusual thing for Jacob to do before going to sleep. The stone's significance emerges not in its use as a headrest but in its metaphorical association with the ladder of Jacob's dream, which connects earth and heaven just as the stone connects Jacob's head and the earth. His astonishment upon awakening centered on his sudden realization of the spiritual power of this particular place, which he later named *Bethel*. The stone connected that heavenly energy directly to Jacob's earthly head as he slept.

Today, a host of new technologies have emerged that can provide unprecedented abilities to influence, manipulate, and control the mind during sleep. Some of these are indeed devices that are to be attached directly to the head. It's a brave new world for those of us who care about the natural wisdom and spiritual autonomy of dreams. The great ethical challenge for big dreamers today is how to use these new tools to help us pursue our goals and how to prevent the tools from being misused or used against us, making us do what other people want in pursuit of their goals. We need to develop technologies that liberate the spirit of dreaming and avoid technologies that imprison and exploit the spirit of dreaming.

Video Representations

New advances in neuroimaging technology are making it possible to use brain data to create video reconstructions of people's dreams while they sleep. Researchers are learning how to observe an awake individual's brain while they are viewing a specific image (let's say a snake) and how to identify neural patterns correlated with that image. Then the researchers observe the individual's brain while sleeping and watch for a recurrence of the "snake" neural pattern. If it appears, a signal can be sent to a video monitor to show an image of a snake—presumably what the sleeping person is dreaming about at that very moment.

This brings within our technological grasp the power to *see into* a person's mind while they are dreaming. Almost immediately, science-fiction visions arise of being able to sit before a screen and watch video representations of our dreams and the dreams of others. To make those visions into realities, many technical challenges will have to be overcome first. Tremendous effort is required to train the algorithms to identify the distinctive patterns of an individual's brain. The patterns for "snake" from my brain will probably not match the "snake" patterns from your brain, so the system needs to be retrained and recalibrated for each individual dreamer. The endless variety of dream content poses another big challenge for this technology. How many different kinds/colors/sizes of snakes need to be built into the system? How many different animals, and plants, and other objects? What about dreams with strange hybrids, unique mixtures, and spontaneous transformations of content: how can those be preprogrammed into the video monitoring system?

Advocates of dream-video technologies emphasize the potential benefits if these challenges can be overcome. For example, researchers would for the first time have truly "objective" dream data, unfiltered by the subjective biases and limited memories of the dreamer. For anyone interested in dreams for personal insight and spiritual guidance, a robust form of dream-video technology would offer a quantum leap in the power to explore one's dreaming experience. It could also be an effective tool in mental health treatment. Psychotherapists would have a powerful new resource for understanding the unconscious conflicts, fears, and concerns of their clients.

These beneficial applications sound appealing, of course. But we should consider just as carefully the potential downsides of this technology—not to block its use but to provide critical feedback for those who are actively working on its development and making important decisions about its design and functionality. Between now and the invention of an actual "dream-viewer," we all should strive for more clarity about several ethical questions such a technology raises.

* Does the process of training and calibrating the system disrupt the natural rhythms of people's sleep and dreams? If yes, what are the long-term health risks and psychological dangers of that disruption? This basic question is too rarely asked in discussions of new dream technologies, perhaps because of an unspoken assumption that dreams themselves aren't really "real," so nothing that harms dreaming does any real harm to a person.
* What is the source of the images used to reconstruct people's dreams? Who chooses those images? Is there transparency in the algorithms that correlate specific images to specific neural patterns? Are measures taken to prevent biases from excluding the appearance of certain kinds of images and favoring others?
* Does the technology distort and flatten the contents of people's dreams? It seems likely a dream-viewer will be incapable of representing bizarre or anomalous experiences for which there are no images. It will struggle to represent essential but non-imagistic elements of dreaming like feelings, thoughts, and bodily sensations. It won't be able to convey intangible qualities of intensity, atmosphere, or awareness. Writer Jorge Luis Borges noted these qualities when he described a nightmare of an ancient king standing by his bed: "Retold, my dream is nothing; dreamt, it was terrible." Will a dream-viewer ever be able to convey the ineffable terror in a nightmare like the one Borges experienced? I have my doubts. Videos will show what videos show, not what dreams *are* in any full or objective sense.
* Who will have access to the dream-viewers? What is done with this incredibly personal source of information? It

takes little imagination to envision potential abuses of this technology for commercial, political, governmental, and/or criminal purposes. The possibility of people with malicious intent gaining access to private details so secret even the individual does not consciously know them: this should be an urgent ethical concern for anyone developing a technology offering an unfiltered view into people's dreams.

* Can this technology be reengineered to manipulate the process and contents of dreaming itself? What if a tool designed to identify neural patterns associated with dreaming could be repurposed to selectively target specific patterns for suppression or stimulation? This seems to lead into the territory of films like *Dreamscape* and *Inception*, where people become vulnerable to an unprecedented depth of external control and manipulation.

* How much dream awareness can people handle? How much is too much? An even more direct movie reference to this kind of technology appears in Wim Wenders's futuristic film *Until the End of the World* (1991), in which the equivalent of a dream-viewer has been invented. In the film, the CIA is determined to steal the device. This is an entirely plausible premise; if and when a dream-viewer is actually created, CIA interrogators will surely be at the front of the line to get one. More unexpectedly, the characters in the movie who use the device become lost within their own nocturnal fantasies. They give up interest in the rest of the world, retreating into the video womb of their reconstructed dreaming. Here, the technology's danger is not abuse by others but our own abuse of it. We might assume that more insight into our

dreams is a good thing, but is that true for everyone? Does each of us have a healthy limit of dream awareness, beyond which we become lost in ourselves?

Tools for Stimulating Dreams

In many cultural contexts and periods of history, people have devised highly effective technologies to evoke special kinds of dreams. Under the general heading of *dream incubation*, these methods include alterations to where and when people sleep, which clothing they wear, which substances they consume, which prayers they recite, how they cleanse themselves, what they offer, and what they sacrifice. The wide variety of these techniques suggests that the effectiveness of dream incubation depends not on any one specific action but on the interplay of many elements. Their combined effect helps to crystallize the individual's intention to be open to a dream that helps them address a concern of real importance in their waking life. This historical background gives us a useful way of evaluating new technologies that aim to stimulate dreams. How much more effective are these new tools than traditional rituals of dream incubation? Do they add anything to the practice?

Maybe they do, and that can be a good thing. A computer program, for example, could provide people with a dream incubation template to follow, helping them figure out which combination of presleep ritual activities are most effective for each individual. Dozens of wearable devices for dream stimulation are already on the market, mostly with the goal of improving people's chances of having a lucid dream. Attached to one's wrist, head, or face, these devices record information while you sleep and then prompt you with chimes, lights, and/or buzzers during preprogrammed times in the sleep cycle in the hope that you will not wake up fully but rather stay asleep while becoming self-aware—"I hear/see/feel the signal from the dream-o-matic; that means I must be dreaming." Note that for devices like this to succeed, the user must formulate the presleep intention to become lucid when hearing the signal. Without that individually created framework of meaning, which connects the stimulus to a self-chosen goal, all the signals, lights, and buzzes will be nothing more than sleep-disturbing annoyances.

I would say something similar about any substance that a person eats, drinks, absorbs, injects, or smokes prior to sleep in hopes of stimulating a powerful dream. Examples of these substances include hallucinogenic plants like ayahuasca, psilocybin, and peyote, along with synthetic drugs like ketamine and galantamine. The ingestion of a sufficient amount of these substances is virtually guaranteed to make a strong impact on how your mind works, both awake and asleep. Based on current research, which has expanded dramatically in recent times, and on personal experience, which goes back many years but made a lasting impression, I can affirm the adage of Timothy Leary: It's always a matter of *set*, *setting*, and *dose*. Whatever it is that you take into your body, the key factors are the quality of your mental and physical preparations (the set), the safety of your location (the setting), and the quantity of what you are consuming relative to your body size and metabolism (the dose). If there is a problem or weakness on any of these fronts, the "trip" can quickly turn in dangerously destabilizing directions.

It is true, as advocates often stress, that ayahuasca, peyote, and other plant-based substances have long histories of safe and beneficial use in traditional cultures. It's also true, as advocates rarely acknowledge, that these uses typically occur within a larger spiritual framework of collective beliefs and practices, not as isolated experiments by novices. The concern here is similar to the one raised in chapter 7 about one's motivation for trying to induce lucidity in dreaming. Before you put a powerful and unpredictable substance into your body, have you taken some time to reflect on the basic question of *why* you want to do this? What are you trying to accomplish that you cannot accomplish in less dangerous ways?

The Reality of Dreaming

When we talk about ethical or unethical actions and behaviors, we usually mean actions and behaviors in the waking world. The ethical status of what happens in our dreams, however, is more difficult to determine, in large part because the answer depends on one's view of the reality status of dreaming. If dreams are not "real," then whatever we do in them is not real either, and no ethical duties or obligations seem to apply. From this perspective, dreaming is an ethical "free-fire zone" with no lasting consequences or significance. If, however, one believes that dreams *are* real in some important sense, then our actions in dreaming do have an ethical dimension to them. This is the perspective of all traditions that look to dreams for spiritual guidance and insight.

Problems arise when people with the former view do things to influence and manipulate the dreams of people with the latter view. This is precisely what happens when commercial advertisers try to use sophisticated dream-stimulating technologies to interject a desire for a product into a person's unconscious mind. Think of it like this: In regular waking life, if someone deceived you into doing something you didn't want to do, that would clearly be unethical on their part. But does that judgment change if the same thing happens in your dreams? If the person deceives you into dreaming of something you would not otherwise dream about, can we still call their action unethical? It seems not, according to the view that nothing that happens in dreaming really matters. Where's the harm? Where's the negative impact? They might have forced you to have a dream, but all dreams are unreal, so what exactly did they force you to do? When we start with the assumption that dreaming is unreal, it becomes more difficult to draw appropriate ethical lines around the use of technologies that have effects on other people's capacity for dreaming.

Ironically, perhaps, support for a higher-reality status for dreaming comes from current scientific research. Findings from cognitive neuroscience have shown that while dreaming, the brain is processing our experiences in almost exactly the same way that it processes our experiences in waking life. The vivid realism of dreaming is deeply rooted in the regular, healthy workings of the neural networks of the sleep cycle. If we look at what the brain is doing during stages of REM sleep, we can see it doing everything it can to generate experiences that feel as "real" as anything in waking life.

Religious traditions have been teaching this same basic idea since ancient times, long before modern science arrived on the scene. Buddhists, for example, believe that karmic traces from earthly attachments can accumulate in sleep; thus, a Buddhist would never look to dreaming as an opportunity to break the precepts and get away with it. Christian theologians like Augustine and Aquinas also argued that if people consent to immoral behavior in their dreams, their souls are indeed responsible for those sins. If a demon attacks you, there's not much you can do, and thus you are not accountable for whatever happens in those dreams. If, however, your sinful behavior gave the devil an opening, then you *are* responsible for the dreaming results.

Modern researchers are adding empirical evidence and a neurocognitive framework to confirm this perennial insight about the ethical significance of dreaming. What happens to us in our dreams *matters*, from both psychological and many religious perspectives. What happens in our dreams has an impact on us, shaping and influencing our waking lives in more ways than we can understand. We can't just say, "What happens in our dreams stays in our dreams." No, what happens in dreaming very definitely goes beyond dreaming into our waking life, whether or not we become self-aware of that process as it unfolds over time.

The Low-Tech Approach

The pace of innovation in this realm is accelerating rapidly. Increasing numbers of technologists and entrepreneurs are recognizing the huge potential market in sleep and dream wearables. In the near future, we can look forward to even more sophisticated dream masks, monitors, and video displays than those available today. I still believe, however, that none of these new technologies is as valuable for the study of dreams as the dream journal. A simple record of an individual's dreams over time: this is still the most powerful tool we have for exploring dreams. Even when compared to the most high-tech devices used by brain scientists, the dream journal has big advantages in effectiveness, accessibility, and privacy.

Effectiveness. The new dream technologies mentioned above have very short track records. We still do not know many important details about their long-term impact on brain functioning during sleep, nor do we know how the impact varies according to individual differences among people from across the demographic spectrum. Plus, many of these tools rely on measurements of neural activity that need to be interpreted by the researchers and translated into meaningful mental content. That is neither an easy nor a purely objective process.

Dream journals as tools of dream exploration, however, have a very long track record, going back many centuries. We know from extensive psychological research that recording one's dreams over time yields rich personal insights and self-knowledge. Only by tracking an individual's dreams over time can these patterns be identified. Both for psychologists doing research and for individuals seeking personal growth, the dream journal remains the most effective technology available.

Accessibility. Many of the latest dream technologies can only be used in hospitals or research laboratories. Some devices have been developed for home use, but they tend to be expensive and complicated to operate. They usually require a smartphone or computer system, plus a reliable internet connection and power source. All of these factors have limited the accessibility of new dream technologies to a fairly small number of people. The dream journal, by contrast, is available to virtually everyone. To keep a dream journal, you need no training or special preparation, and you don't have to go to a laboratory or hospital. All that is required is a method of recording your dreams (e.g., pen and paper) and a safe place to preserve them over time. This makes the dream journal by far the most accessible tool for studying dreams.

Privacy. Almost every type of new dream technology has connections to the internet that feed data from individual dreamers to the researchers and back again. Even if the researchers preserve the confidentiality of the individual's data—which, of course, they should—the mere presence of an outsider peering into one's dreams naturally heightens people's concerns about personal privacy. Some of the new technologies—for example, dream-visualization tools and dream-altering substances—clearly raise enormous ethical issues around protecting the privacy and integrity of a person's inner thoughts.

A dream journal, on the other hand, is essentially a personal diary. A dream journal "works" without anyone else's input. All you need is you, paying attention to your own dreams consistently over time. You can keep the results to yourself, and no one else needs to know anything about what you are doing.

None of this is to dismiss the exciting potentials of many new technologies to improve our understanding of dreams and perhaps even enhance our experience of dreaming in a meaningful way. But the enduring power and elegance of the dream journal, and its advantages in effectiveness, accessibility, and privacy, suggest that a good strategy for new technologies is to build on the dream journal, amplifying what it can already do. Any new dream technology will be stronger if it is grafted onto a solid dream journal system as its roots.

One of the earliest empirical dream researchers, Mary Whiton Calkins, performed a quantitative study of two dream journals, her own and that of a colleague. She published the results in 1893 in the *American Journal of Psychology*. Although she is rarely acknowledged for her pioneering work, Calkins identified many of the basic patterns of dream form and content that later generations of researchers have essentially confirmed. And what were the technologies Calkins used for her study? Her method, she said, "Was very simple: to record each night, immediately after waking from a dream, every remembered feature of it. For this purpose, paper, pencil, candle, and matches were placed close at hand."

The Sleep and Dream Database

This low-tech method—keeping a dream journal to help with dream recall and meaning-making—is more than just advice I give to others. It's the foundation for my own work with the SDDb, the online archive of dream reports and survey data about sleep and dreaming that I mentioned earlier. The driving question behind the SDDb was this: if dreams truly have meaningful patterns of content, what is the best way to identify them?

When I began keeping my own dream journal, I learned from firsthand experience that many aspects of dream content can be identified and tabulated fairly easily—characters, for example, and colors, and references to flying and falling. I also learned that it can be very tedious and time-consuming to go through hundreds of dream reports, trying to count all these different items of content. The Hall and Van de Castle system of content analysis can make this process more systematic, but it does not eliminate the labor-intensive demands of categorizing the contents of a large collection of dreams, such as those found in an individual's long-term journal. For much of the twentieth century, the task of dream coding often fell to graduate students, who served a portion of their apprenticeship as psychology researchers by learning the Hall and Van de Castle system and applying it to new sets of dream reports.

This began to change in the 1990s. The Dreambank.net website, developed by G. William Domhoff and Adam Schneider, was an early version that made a big impact on my awareness of the potentials in this realm. My academic background was in the humanities and social sciences—very far from anything having to do with database technologies. In my early writings, I had sharply criticized the Hall and Van de Castle system for its quantified approach to the meaning of dreams. I could see countless problems, failings, and limitations in the ways other researchers were applying this system. Even then, however, I had to admit I saw some interesting possibilities here—at least if the system were used less heavy-handedly and with more attention to how the statistical results might relate to the qualitative dimensions of dreaming. After several years of working with Domhoff and Schneider and the resources of the Dreambank, in 2009 I developed the SDDb, with the help of data scientist Kurt Bollacker. Like the Dreambank, the SDDb is free and open-access, meaning all the data and all the analytic tools are available for study by anyone with an internet connection. This is meant to stimulate conversation and encourage new people to become involved in dream research, people who come from a wider variety of backgrounds than has ever been possible before.

For several years, I had been developing a method to identify meaningful patterns in people's dreams by using the statistical frequencies of word usage in their dreams. If I can look at one hundred dreams from a person, for example, and analyze their dreams using the word search tools of the SDDb, I can generate a statistical profile of that person's dream world that suggests a variety of predictions about their concerns in waking life. If the person dreams far more often of their father than their mother, we can infer that their father is more emotionally important to them in waking life than their mother is. This prediction is based on the continuity hypothesis: that the frequency of something's appearance in dreaming accurately indicates how important it is in waking life. The statistical analysis also reveals unusual and anomalous features of a person's dreams, which can prompt further predictions. For instance, if the person rarely dreams of death, the few dreams in which death *does* occur may have special significance. This prediction is based on the discontinuity hypothesis: that rare elements of content can express deeply important meanings, often relating to the person's religious or spiritual outlook on life.

With the help of Bill Domhoff, I performed several experiments using this basic approach. He would send me a set of dreams from someone I did not know; I would analyze the dreams and make inferences about the person's waking-life concerns, which I then sent back to Domhoff, who would forward them to the dreamer for comment and correction. Most of my inferences were confirmed as correct by the dreamers (75 percent or higher). This was all the more remarkable since I never even read their actual dreams but relied strictly on the frequency of word usage to make the predictions. In other words, I pretended to be a robot, focusing on numbers and only numbers.

I probably could have reached an even higher percentage of correct inferences if I had gone ahead and read the actual dreams. But the point of the experiment was to see how much accurate information could be derived solely from the quantitative analysis, without a human interpreter who could draw additional meanings from the narrative texts of the dreams. What can the numbers alone tell us? The answer is a lot. A *lot* a lot. The strongest signals of meaning that appeared in these studies included relationships with family members and other people, daily activities, emotional temperament, sexual behavior, cultural interests, and religious background.

The first big lesson I learned in these experiments was to develop a better bedside manner when delivering my inferences to the dreamer. Initially, I shared the analytical results and the predictions about their waking lives without any context or elaboration. Many of the dreamers reacted with surprise and even shock at what I was able to learn about their lives without ever having met them. Even though they were informed participants—people who had consented to the process and who ultimately found the results valuable and personally meaningful—they still experienced a startling moment of self-discovery, one mediated by another person: namely, me and my database. I realized that at a certain point in the process, I needed to stop being a robot and think again as a human, imagining how the dreamer might respond emotionally to the various inferences and how I might deliver the ideas with a bit more empathy and human concern.

Dream Interpretation Put to the Test

A few years ago, my friend and colleague Deirdre Barrett of Harvard Medical School suggested we try a live demonstration of this method at an upcoming dream studies conference. She would provide me with a large set of dreams from an individual—who had agreed, of course—and I would analyze the dreams and make some predictions about the person's concerns in waking life. The twist was that this would happen as a conference presentation, after which the dreamer would stand up from the audience, come to the podium, and respond to my predictions. I would find out if my inferences were accurate or not in front of a large crowd of my professional peers. This would be an experimental dream interpretation as a high-wire act—without a net!

The conference was hosted at a meeting center in a beautiful medieval structure in a rural part of the Netherlands. Traveling to the site was long and exhausting, and on the morning of my presentation, I woke up feeling worse than I ever remembered feeling—I must have been at a point of maximal jet-lagged discombobulation. The mere thought of standing in front of a large group of professional colleagues for approximately one hour made my stomach lurch and my head spin alarmingly. I gave up on going to breakfast and just lay quietly with my eyes closed, hoping my mind and body would somehow renew their acquaintance with each other.

A few minutes before the presentation began, I got out of bed, put on my clothes and name badge, walked gingerly to the session room, set my papers on the podium, and started speaking. If this unusual experiment was going to flop, at least I would be too fuzzy to care.

I began by explaining that our experiment involved the "blind" interpretation of an individual's dream series using a digital method of analysis that focuses on word usage frequencies. This method is blind because it brackets out all external knowledge about the dreamer and their personal life. Only the word usage frequencies are factored into the interpretation. The essence of the approach is its minimalism: it aims to get the most meaning from the least amount of data. It relies on very simple and objective information—objective in the sense that anyone who analyzes the same set of dreams will count the same number of words used in the reports. I also emphasized that this approach does not provide all relevant answers to all questions about dreams. It is very good at answering some questions and utterly useless at answering others. We're still trying to figure out how to make more progress with the former and not waste time with the latter.

I told the attendees how this would work. All I knew was the dreamer was a woman, an avid journal-keeper since 1985, who had consented to this process and who was planning to attend the conference. A few weeks earlier, Deirdre had sent me the dreams of Brianna (the pseudonym we agreed to use), which amounted to approximately twenty-five hundred total reports. I uploaded these reports into the SDDb and then applied a word search template I have been developing, which has forty categories of words covering several areas of dream content: perceptions, characters, emotions, social interactions, cultural references, and others. I then compared the results with the SDDb female baselines, a macro set of 3,095 "most recent" dream reports from a variety of sources. The baselines provide a kind of measuring stick for evaluating the content frequencies of average, ordinary dreams.

Given the limitations of time, I decided to look at three subsets of dreams from three separate time periods, not the whole series of twenty-five hundred, which would have taken too long to process in time for the presentation. This was not really a disadvantage, however, since the three subsets gave us a chance to look for meaningful patterns across three different times in the dreamer's life. Domhoff and I had done something similar in previous experiments—looking at continuities and disconti-nuities in dream content frequencies from different periods of time—and the results had been encouraging.

Before going on with the analysis, I made a point of acknowl-edging the human dimension of the project. "I want to pause for a moment and thank the dreamer, somewhere out in the audi-ence, for her profound dedication to her own dreaming imagi-nation, which is very impressive, and for her willingness to share the treasure of her dream journal with us, which is incredibly generous and so valuable for everyone interested in the empirical study of dreams," I said. "It's an amazing gift, so thanks to the dreamer!" If I had my wits more about me, I could have scanned the faces of the audience to see if I could spot a reaction from the likely dreamer, but at this moment, just standing and not toppling over was taking up all my attention.

A total of nineteen inferences emerged from the analysis. Some of the predictions involved general patterns across all Brianna's dreams, and some of the predictions related more to one time period of dreams than the others. Again, this is still very new and experimental research, with lots of trial-and-error methodology, so everything will hopefully become more precise as other researchers and I develop more sophisticated ways of applying these tools of analysis.

So here is what robot-me identified in the statistical frequencies of Brianna's dreams. First, I noted, the dreamer is a female. I already knew this, so I did not include it in the numbered list below. Still, it was important to note that other frequencies in her dreams (her high proportion of anxiety, family characters, and friendly interactions) reliably distinguish female from male dreamers. Even if I had *not* known Brianna was female, the word usage patterns would have accurately told me the same thing.

1. Fear and anxiety are a concern for the dreamer, especially in set 2, much less in set 3 (her frequencies of fear-related words were much higher than the female baselines—almost half her dreams have some reference to feelings of anxiety).
2. She is closer to her mother than her father (more mother than father references).
3. She is unlikely to be married (few references to husband, wife, marriage, etc.).
4. She is unlikely to have a child (few references to babies, children, etc.).
5. She is not a dog or cat owner (few references to domestic animals).

6. She is not a videogame player (few references to fantastic beings or to flying and falling).

7. She is a friendly, socially engaged person (high proportion of friendly social interactions, numerous characters).

8. She frequently has nightmares of violence and physical aggression, although much less in set 3 (high frequencies of anxiety, physical aggression, and death in sets 1 and especially 2, less in 3).

9. She is sexually active, more so in set 1 (higher frequency of sexual interactions in set 1 compared to sets 2 and 3).

10. Death is a concern for her, especially in set 2, less in set 3 (unusually high frequencies of references to death).

11. She is cognitively alert, active (high frequencies of references to thinking, social interactions).

12. She is verbal, talkative (high frequency of references to speech).

13. Books are important to her, and writing is too (high frequency of references to reading and writing).

14. She has a higher education, or is in school at least at a university level, especially in set 2 (high frequency of school references).

15. She works a lot, perhaps has a job at an office (high frequency of work and job references).

16. She likes art and is actively engaged with it; more music in set 1; more poetry in sets 2 and 3 (high frequency of references to arts in general and these arts in particular).

17. The Jewish religion plays a significant role in her life (high frequency of Jewish-related words in the religion word search category).

18. She is not interested in sports (few references to sports).

As soon as I finished, I aimed for the nearest chair, where I collapsed in exhaustion and awaited my fate.

Deirdre then invited Brianna to come forward, and she proceeded to give a wonderfully insightful and generous response to my inferences—sixteen of eighteen of which turned out to be correct. Listening to Brianna, I began to perk up. I hung on her every word, fascinated to hear from the live human being whose voluminous, richly detailed dreams I had up to that point treated as nothing more than mathematical abstractions. It turned out she was an accomplished scholar in her own right, impressively bright and eloquent. I was also relieved that she was clearly a stable, mature person who truly enjoyed the project and was comfortable talking about her personal life. As I said earlier, the impact of a blind analysis process can be startling and rather intense. Deirdre, a therapist herself, had assured me that Brianna understood what we were doing and would be fine with receiving my thoughts about her dreams' connection to her life. Still, I was very glad to hear it directly from her.

A couple of my inferences about her waking life missed the mark. My use of the word "closer" to characterize her relationship with her mother versus her father was too vague for her to confirm. Brianna said she has very different relationships with her parents, close in some ways and not in others. My inference was clearly anticipating a more binary situation, so I'd have to count this one as incorrect.

Brianna also said that while she does not have any biological children, she does have an adopted daughter, to whom she refers in the dreams by her proper name. My analysis did not include any searches for proper names, so this important aspect of Brianna's waking life eluded me.

But other than that, she confirmed the other sixteen inferences (plus the one about being female) were correct. She shared some highly relevant information about the personal life experiences that shaped the varying patterns of her dreams over the course of the three time periods covered by my analysis.

As the conversation with the rest of the audience unfolded, several interesting points emerged. I was especially intrigued by the continuities between her dreams and her cultural interests. She had unusually high frequencies of references to art, religion, and reading and writing, much higher than the female baselines, and these variations correlated with her active engagement in all these areas in waking life. Brianna had recently completed a graduate degree in creative writing. She had published both poetry and academic articles, and she owned a large personal collection of books. Although she does have a Jewish cultural background, Brianna's concerns with religion and spirituality were even greater and more wide-ranging than I had inferred, and in the group discussion she noted several dreams about her meaningful interactions with Buddhism, Christianity, and other spiritual traditions. Overall, I took this as strong validation of the idea that dreams accurately express a person's cultural interests, preferences, and activities.

The biggest insight centered on the significant shift from the second to the third set of her dreams in their references to fear, physical aggression, and death. Brianna felt comfortable acknowledging that earlier in life, including the time periods of sets 1 and 2 of her dreams, she had experiences of people dying, being threatened with death herself, and working in a nongovernmental organization focused on human rights abuses in developing countries. The many nightmares of violence she suffered in these years had an ample basis in the realities of her waking life.

At a certain point, these bad dreams changed, however, and Brianna said it was due to a very specific reason: she began a psychotherapy process that felt meaningful and effective. Because of the help she received in therapy, the nightmares and anxiety-laden dreams diminished to a much more moderate and emotionally manageable level. Brianna herself identified the key implication here when she pointed out during the discussion that dreams could serve as an indicator of the progress and effectiveness of a psychotherapeutic treatment.

That, potentially, is a very big deal.

Serving the Dreamer

The prospect arises here of a digital dream-journaling tool for psychotherapy clients to record their dreams in a database system. The database could automatically provide a preliminary analysis and interpretation, giving clients and their therapists a wealth of new material to explore during their sessions together. Sounds exciting, right? It's going to happen—and sooner rather than later too. The technology exists right now to create such a system, and the tools will only become more powerful over time.

The challenge is to make sure that analytic systems like these are designed to serve the interests of the *dreamer*, first and foremost. This should be the cardinal principle for any technology that aims to influence or shape people's experiences with dreams: to keep the dreamer's concerns at the center of the process. Unfortunately, we do not always see that principle honored in the areas of dream videos and dream stimulation, where attention seems more focused on what can be done *to* the dreamer rather than what the technologies are doing in any positive, helpful way *for* the dreamer. Dream videos have some appeal for personal use, but the excitement driving much of the research in this area comes from the hope of gaining a third-person perspective on dreaming—in other words, being able to watch someone else's dreams while they are happening.

I can imagine virtuous dream-video systems being developed in accordance with the core principle of serving the dreamer's interests, but I can just as easily imagine various ways of abusing these systems for criminal, commercial, political, or military purposes. The same is true with dream-stimulating technologies, which are designed to be used voluntarily but in the wrong circumstances could be applied involuntarily to people whose dreams would be manipulated for malevolent purposes. And to push the point further, I would question the assumption that people are "voluntarily" seeking tools to stimulate dreams. In a society that prizes the values of control and power, it's quite easy to sell a product that promises new opportunities to exercise control and power. The fact that the product involves dreaming is secondary and ultimately irrelevant to what is really being bought and sold. The purchase of the device, substance, or program may be voluntary, but it's still doubtful the interests of the *dreamer* are truly being served.

And if a culture becomes permeated with dream-impacting technologies that serve the interests of people *other* than the dreamers, it is no longer just a personal problem; it now becomes a threat to the health and spiritual vitality of the whole community. Dreaming is an innate, evolutionarily hardwired function of the human brain during sleep. It is also an experience that people from around the world and all through history have considered profoundly important, meaningful, and useful in their waking lives. Any new technology that has the potential, whether intended or not, to disrupt the natural rhythms of people's sleep and dreaming needs to be publicly evaluated in terms of its long-term risks and benefits. In that context, the lowly dream journal, enhanced by digital databases, will remain for the foreseeable future the most powerful, effective, and ethically sound technology for helping dreamers better understand their dreams. Other than a rock from Bethel.

CONCLUSION

It's possible I have made things worse, not better, with the idea that dreaming is a kind of play. The connection to play does little to make dreams appear less trivial or frivolous. In fact, it risks making them look even more like an escape from our collective problems and a distraction from serious efforts to solve those problems. At a time when apocalyptic threats are looming in all directions, how can we justify paying attention to the "spirit of play" in dreaming?

The question itself reflects a culture that has fallen dangerously out of touch with its own dreaming resources. As we have learned from many areas of study—from history and anthropology, art and religion, neuroscience and digital technology—dreams are a natural and healthy part of human life. They reflect the powers of the imagination inherent in all people, and they actively enhance our flexibility, resilience, and adaptiveness in the waking world. This is still true today, whether or not we choose to acknowledge it. People throughout history and in all cultures have celebrated dreaming as a special means of revelatory insight that is accessible to everyone, regardless of their social status or waking-life circumstances. The spiritual dynamism of dreaming infuses individuals and their communities with energies of movement, change, growth, and transformation. Grounding people in the past and orienting them toward the future, dreams look beyond the artificial limits of present reality to envision new and better possibilities for the future. *Especially* in times of crisis—*especially* when apocalyptic threats are looming on all sides—that's when our capacity for dreaming becomes most relevant to waking life, both individually and collectively. That's when dreaming emerges as a deeply rooted emergency response system within every individual that can guide us through frightening situations of crisis, conflict, and vulnerability to forces beyond our control. And that's when big dreamers, with their heightened oneiric sensitivities, become especially valuable to their communities.

Where Will You Go from Here?

The playful creativity of your sleeping mind makes it impossible to predict what exactly you will dream on any given night. In this sense, the creative spontaneity of dreaming provides nightly evidence of our spiritual freedom. The sheer fact of our endlessly varied experiences of dreaming refutes a deterministic, mechanical view of the world. In dreams, we glimpse our true autonomy as beings who always have the capacity to grow, change, and imagine. Your waking life may feel tightly bound, constrained, and limited, but dreaming will always remind you of the open-ended vistas of spiritual growth unfolding before you.

Although I cannot predict the contents of your next dream, I can make some educated guesses about the future patterns of your dreams over time. Going forward, your dreaming will probably follow the major currents of most people's dreams in that you will frequently dream of being with your friends and family, in familiar places, doing familiar things. You will probably have slightly more negative dreams than positive ones, with more falling than flying and more misfortunes than good fortunes. White, black, and red will be your most frequently appearing colors. The emotional qualities of your dreams will frequently mirror your emotions in waking life. Whatever you most care about in the day, you will likely dream about at night.

You will also have dreams that deviate dramatically from these baseline patterns of common dream content. Your dreams will change whenever something important and meaningful happens to you, whenever you are startled or decentered in a fundamental way. When your waking life brings you new struggles and challenges, your dreams will change in response to highlight the vital issues at stake and in some cases to anticipate their future unfolding. When you suffer a serious blow—a deep disappointment, a traumatizing loss—your dreams will change in response to guide you forward on the path of healing. When big upheavals happen in your community—a political crisis, or a natural disaster—your dreams will change in response to help you and others make sense of the new reality. When you shift your waking attention to focus on your inner world—by meditation or prayer, by journaling or taking a solitary walk in the woods—your dreams will change in response to welcome the integration of conscious and unconscious perspectives. When you talk with other people about dreams—in a formal dream-sharing group or in a brief, random conversation with a stranger—your dreams will change in response to help you connect more fully with your spiritual potentials and the spiritual potentials in all people.

Let me close with a story about one of the early lessons I learned about the power of shared dreaming. Many years ago, I taught a class on dreams as part of an adult education program in a big city. The students were a diverse group of people in their thirties and forties who worked in various jobs—marketing, real estate, restaurants—and simply wanted to learn more about dreams for their own personal enlightenment. The class met one evening per week, and at the start of each session, the students let out a collective sigh of relief; the workday was done, and now they looked forward to a couple of hours of nourishment for their minds and souls. In the first half of each class, we discussed the readings for the week, and in the second half, we shared dreams with each other, using the basic method we looked at in chapter 3. Every group of students creates its own little cultural dynamic, its own unspoken sense of who is in the group and how we relate to each other. In this class, I noticed that after just the first two meetings, an older, rather quiet woman named Claire had become the calming center of the group. She wasn't the quickest or best-read student in the class, but whenever she spoke, everyone listened intently and took her words to heart.

We usually had time to talk about one or two people's dreams per week, so it wasn't until the fourth meeting that we had a chance to hear a dream from Claire. She told us about a recurrent dream of being caught in a tidal wave. In her dream, she is standing at the beach, facing the ocean, and she sees a massive wave rise up before her, threatening to crash down upon her. But instead of running away or resisting, Claire calmly stands her ground and lets the wave wash over her, letting it pass and emerging safely from the water.

After she finished, everyone in the group sat silently for a moment and marveled at this dream. It accurately reflected what we knew of Claire's unflappable personality, and yet it also seemed magical and astonishing, almost superhuman. Who could remain unmoving in front of a vast, surging wall of water, serenely trusting in their ultimate safety? As I mentioned to the class, giant tidal waves are a recurrent nightmare theme for many people, often reflecting a feeling that forces in the waking world are threatening to overwhelm us. The psychologist Ernest Hartmann often spoke of tidal wave dreams as a classic example of a nightmare image that expresses a deep, existential feeling of vulnerability. The other students in the class were just as intrigued as I was by the Claire's unusual dream, which seemed to defy that profound vulnerability with an equally profound courage.

A couple of weeks later, another student, Marianne, excitedly asked to share a dream during the second half of class. She was a much more anxious and high-strung person than Claire. Although she always made good, insightful comments during class discussion, I could tell Marianne was also carrying a lot of internal stress and self-doubt. But now she had a dream to share that seemed to fill her with a very different kind of energy.

Here is what she told us: She is standing at the seashore, looking out at the ocean, when suddenly a huge tidal wave rises up and threatens to crash upon her. She turns and starts to run away but then stops. She slowly turns around and stands facing the water. She says to herself, "When the tidal wave came in Claire's dream, she didn't run; she stood right where she was, and it turned out okay. So that's what I'll do." The wave crashes down on Marianne and consumes her, but she remains calm, trusting in the example of Claire's dream to save her. A moment later, Marianne awoke, filled with relief and wonder. Upon hearing this in class, the other students—including Claire—were delighted. Claire recognized and appreciated the sincere oneiric compliment.

Moments like this provide the building blocks for a healthier culture of dreaming. Claire's willingness to share her dream, and Marianne's willingness to listen to it and imagine it as her own, led to a surprisingly meaningful shift in Marianne's awareness and a beautiful illustration of the self-transforming and *other-transforming* power that lies within each dreamer. *We do not only dream for ourselves:* That may sound paradoxical to Western ears, but it's a vital truth about the spiritual essence of dreaming. The more deeply you explore your dreams, the more you realize they are not really "your" dreams at all. They are the dreams of the spirit of life itself manifesting within your sleeping mind. Can you recognize this emergent power within yourself? Within all humans? Perhaps within all animate beings?

It's a simple idea with far-reaching consequences. Think about that while you're falling asleep tonight. Dream well!

NOTES

Chapter 1

"When we are asleep": Arianna Huffington, *The Sleep Revolution: Transforming Your Life One Night at a Time* (New York: Harmony, 2016), 12.

"Their discoveries of molecular mechanisms": Nobel Press Release. https://www.nobelprize.org/prizes/medicine/2017/press-release/.

"We are born with a strong circadian clock": Satchin Panda, *The Circadian Code* (New York: Rodale, 2018), xv, 45.

"Basic hospitality of the same order": Roger Ivar Lohmann, "Sleeping among the Asabano: Surprises in Intimacy and Sociality at the Margins of Consciousness," in *Sleep around the World: Anthropological Perspectives*, ed. Katie Glaskin and Richard Chenhall (New York: Palgrave Macmillan, 2013), 28.

"Whenever there was some kind of stress": Lohmann, "Sleeping among the Asabano," 32.

Most adults do well with seven to nine hours of sleep: "How Much Sleep Do We Really Need?" Sleep Foundation, August 29, 2022, https://www.sleepfoundation.org/how-sleep-works/how-much -sleep-do-we-really-need.

Sleep researcher William Dement of Stanford University: William Dement and Christopher Vaughan, *The Promise of Sleep* (New York: Dell, 1999).

Sleep deprivation is a public health issue: Tricia Hersey, *Rest Is Resistance: A Manifesto* (New York: Little, Brown Spark, 2022), 18.

Studies suggest that insomnia: Kelly Bulkeley and Michael Schredl, "Dreams, Race, and the Black Lives Matter Movement: Results of a Survey of American Adults," *Pastoral Psychology* 71 (2022): 29–41.

We believe rest is a form of resistance: "About," https://thenapministry. wordpress.com/about/; and "Rest Is Anything That Connects Your Mind and Body," The Nap Ministry, February 21, 2022, https:// thenapministry.wordpress.com/2022/02/21/rest-is-anything-that -connects-your-mind-and-body/.

Chapter 2

On the contrary, church authorities went out of their way: Morton Kelsey, *God, Dreams, and Revelation: A Christian Interpretation of Dreams* (Minneapolis: Augsburg Press, 1991).

A small percentage (around 8 percent): Kelly Bulkeley, *Big Dreams: The Science of Dreaming and the Origins of Religion* (New York: Oxford University Press, 2016), 77–94.

For instance, psychoanalyst Ernest Hartmann's research: Ernest Hartmann, R. Elkin, and M. Garg, "Personality and Dreaming: The Dreams of People with Very Thick or Very Thin Boundaries," *Dreaming* 1 (1991), 311–324.

"Openness to experience": Michael Schredl et al., "Dream Recall Frequency, Attitude towards Dreams and Openness to Experience," *Dreaming* 13 (2003): 145–153.

People remember a wide variety: Harry Hunt, *The Multiplicity of Dreams: Memory, Imagination, and Consciousness* (New Haven, CT: Yale University Press, 1989).

"Big dreams are often remembered for a lifetime": C. G. Jung, *Dreams* (Princeton, NJ: Princeton University Press, 1974), 76.

"But if dreams produce such essential compensations": Jung, *Dreams*, 80.

Rather than expecting dreams to make sense: James Hillman, *The Dream and the Underworld* (New York: Harper and Row, 1979).

The metaphor system plays a generative role: George Lakoff, "How Metaphor Structures Dreams: The Theory of Conceptual Metaphor Applied to Dream Analysis," *Dreaming* 3 (1993): 86.

NOTES

Expanding on this research: Jeannette Marie Mageo, *Dreaming Culture: Meanings, Models, and Power in U.S. American Dreams* (New York: Palgrave Macmillan, 2011).

To this day, they remain one: John McDargh was the first secretary-treasurer of the Psychology, Culture, and Religion Group, a program unit of the American Academy of Religion, starting in 1974 until I succeeded him in 1995.

Chapter 3

"When the multiple intelligences and intuitions": Jeremy Taylor, *Dream Work* (Mahwah, NJ: Paulist Press, 1983), 76.

According to survey research I have done: Kelly Bulkeley and Michael Schredl, "Attitudes towards Dreaming: Effects of Socio-demographic and Religious Variables in an American Sample," *International Journal of Dream Research* 12 (2019): 75–81.

In Freud's memorable phrase: Sigmund Freud, *The Interpretation of Dreams*, trans. James Strachey (New York: Avon Books, 1965), 647.

Their group interpretations focus on: Mubuy Mubay Mpier, "Dreams among the Yansi," in *Dreaming, Religion, and Society in Africa*, ed. M. C. Jedrej and Rosalind Shaw (Leiden: E. J. Brill, 1992), 100–110.

What began as an expression: Laura Graham, "Dreams," *Journal of Linguistic Anthropology* 9 (1999): 61–64.

"The Kukatja world is filled with malevolent spirits": Sylvie Poirier, *A World of Relationships: Itineraries, Dreams, and Events in the Australian Western Desert* (Toronto: University of Toronto Press, 2005), 116.

By sharing his dream with others: Clifford E. Trafzer and Margery A. Beach, "Smohalla, the Washani, and Religion as a Factor in Northwestern Indian History," *American Indian Quarterly* 9 (1985): 309–324. For more on Smohalla, see Steven Charleston, *We Survived the End of the World: Lessons from Native America on Apocalypse and Hope* (Minneapolis: Broadleaf Books, 2023).

"It was her use of dreams and visions": Mechal Sobel, *Teach Me Dreams: The Search for Self in the Revolutionary Era* (Princeton, NJ: Princeton University Press, 2000), 230.

NOTES

I was ready to give up: Quoted in Patricia M. Davis, "Discerning the
Voice of God: Case Studies in Christian History," in *Dreaming in
Christianity and Islam: Culture, Conflict, and Creativity,* ed. Kelly
Bulkeley, Kate Adams, and Patricia M. Davis (New Brunswick: Rut-
gers University Press, 2009), 52.
"He seems to be deliberately leaving": Davis, "Discerning the Voice of
God," 52.
The Rev. Martin Luther King, Jr. told his congregation: Davis, "Discerning
the Voice of God," 53.
"It seems clear that leaderless and lay-led": Taylor, *Dream Work,* 77.
"One of the reasons why group dream work is so rewarding": Taylor,
Dream Work, 96.

Chapter 4

I was facing north, and fell asleep: Lee Irwin, "Sending a Voice, Seeking
a Place: Visionary Traditions among Native Women of the Plains," in
*Dreams: A Reader on the Religious, Cultural, and Psychological Dimen-
sions of Dreaming,* ed. Kelly Bulkeley (New York: Palgrave Macmillan,
1999), 104.
Current research in content analysis: Mary Whiton Calkins, "Statistics
of Dreams," *American Psychologist* 5 (1893): 311–343.
"The animal percent . . . is always higher": G. William Domhoff,
Finding Meaning in Dreams: A Quantitative Approach (New York:
Plenum, 1996), 119.
"Because these small-scale societies": Domhoff, *Finding Meaning in
Dreams,* 120.
"The biggest difference between child and adult dreams": Domhoff,
Finding Meaning in Dreams, 89.
"Pregnancy was easy and joyful": Bei Linda Tang, *Navigate Life with
Dreams: A Guide to Happiness and Peace by Working with Your Own
Dreams* (Vancouver: Independently published, 2019), 17.
In this dream I was hanging: Tang, *Navigate Life with Dreams,* 18.
"A high-spirited happy dream": Tang, *Navigate Life with Dreams,* 26.

To form what Linda called a "storyline": Tang, *Navigate Life with Dreams*, 26.

"Having AIDS certainly has put me into contact": Michael Dupré, "Russia. Dreaming. Liberation," *Dreaming* 2 (1992): 123–134.

"I dream that I'm in my room": Dupré, "Russia. Dreaming. Liberation," 125–126.

"It seemed that everyone related to bugs": Dupré, "Russia. Dreaming. Liberation," 126.

"The main metaphor for me was": Dupré, "Russia. Dreaming. Liberation," 126.

A number of years ago: Herbert W. Schroeder, "Seeking the Balance: Do Dreams Have a Role in Natural Resource Management?" in *Among All These Dreamers: Essays on Dreaming and Modern Society*, ed. Kelly Bulkeley (Albany: State University of New York Press, 1996), 36.

"The reason for this condition was a fear": Schroeder, "Seeking the Balance," 36.

They hissed with their ears back: Mary Carskadon, ed., *Encyclopedia of Sleep and Dreaming* (New York: Macmillan, 1993), 48.

"Our collective error was not": David Peña-Guzmán, *When Animals Dream: The Hidden World of Animal Consciousness* (Princeton, NJ: Princeton University Press, 2022), 20.

"Sometimes they also made facial grimaces": Peña-Guzmán, *When Animals Dream*, 124.

"I do not myself know": Sigmund Freud, *The Interpretation of Dreams* (New York: Dell, 1965), 165.

"The discovery of oneiric behaviors in this group": Peña-Guzmán, *When Animals Dream*, 55.

Chapter 5

"It is in dreams that one can": Paul Ricoeur, *The Symbolism of Evil* (Boston: Beacon Press, 1967), 12.

"The symbol gives rise to thought": Ricoeur, *The Symbolism of Evil*, 12.

Real dream vision is an awareness: W. J. Wallace, "The Dream in Mohave Life," *Journal of American Folklore* 60 (1947): 252–258.

For instance, the Mohave people: W. J. Wallace, "The Dream in Mohave Life," *Journal of American Folklore* 60 (1947): 252–258.

Ordinary, everyday dreams: Thomas Gregor, "'Far, Far Away My Shadow Wandered . . .': The Dream Symbolism and Dream Theories of the Mehinaku Indians of Brazil," *American Ethnologist* 8 (1981): 709–720.

They considered a rare few dreams: Craighill Handy, "Dreaming in Relation to Spirit Kindred and Sickness in Hawaii," in *Essays in Anthropology Presented to A. L. Kroeber,* ed. R. H. Lowie (Freeport, TX: Books for Libraries Press, 1936), 119–127.

I care nothing about visions and dreams: Quoted in Bulkeley, *Spiritual Dreaming,* 164.

"Dreams that continued to influence their thoughts": Don Kuiken et al., "The Influence of Impactful Dreams on Self-Perceptual Depth and Spiritual Transformation," *Dreaming* 16 (2006): 259.

"I find myself in a large white room": Bonnelle Lewis Strickling, *Dreaming about the Divine* (Albany: State University of New York Press, 2007), 109.

"I woke with a wonderful feeling": Strickling, *Dreaming about the Divine,* 110.

"It is the face of his own evil shadow": C. G. Jung, *Man and His Symbols* (New York: Dell, 1964), 73.

"You taught me language": *The Tempest,* I.ii. 363–365.

"I'll yield him thee asleep": *The Tempest,* III.ii. 64–65.

"Be not afeard": *The Tempest,* III.iii. 140–148.

"This thing of darkness": *The Tempest,* V.i. 275.

Chapter 6

As anthropologist Ernest Becker observed years ago: Ernest Becker, *The Denial of Death* (New York: Free Press, 1973).

I will share some ideas from a book: Kelly Bulkeley and Patricia Bulkley, *Dreaming beyond Death: A Guide to Pre-Death Dreams and Visions* (Boston: Beacon Press, 2006).

These gods, Hesiod wrote: Hesiod, *Theogony*, trans. Dorothea Wender (New York: Penguin Books, 1973), 211–212.

"In the Tibetan Buddhist literature": Francisco J. Varela, ed., *Sleeping, Dreaming, and Dying: An Exploration of Consciousness with the Dalai Lama* (Somerville, MA: Wisdom Publications, 1997), 49.

"As while you are asleep": Quoted in Bulkeley, *Spiritual Dreaming*, 80–81.

"By whom was he": Quoted in Bulkeley, *Spiritual Dreaming*, 80–81.

Most participants reported experiencing: Christopher W. Kerr et al., "End-of-Life Dreams and Visions: A Longitudinal Study of Hospice Patients' Experiences," *Journal of Palliative Medicine* 17 (2014): 296–303.

Talk to any long-term care staff: Jeanne Van Brockhorst, *Dreaming at the Threshold: Guidance, Comfort, and Healing at the End of Life* (Woodbury, NY: Llewellyn, 2015), 80–81.

Chapter 7

"Then this person becomes self-illuminated": *Upanishads*, trans. Patrick Olivelle (New York: Oxford University Press, 1996), 59.

This might sound like a surprisingly modern theory: G. William Domhoff, *The Neurocognitive Theory of Dreaming* (Cambridge: MIT Press, 2022).

"Catching the big fish": David Lynch, *Catching the Big Fish: Meditation, Consciousness, and Creativity* (Los Angeles: Jeremy Tarcher, 2007).

On pulling up the blind: Celia Greene, *Lucid Dreams* (Oxford: Institute for Psychophysical Research, 1968), 86, 105.

During the day I had the sensation: Lobsang P. Lhalungpa, *The Life of Milarepa* (Boston: Shambhala, 1985), 129.

"Shortly thereafter Reid stopped remembering": Quoted in Bulkeley, *Spiritual Dreaming*, 83.

"Self-reflectiveness scale": Sheila Purcell, Alan Moffitt, and Robert Hoffmann, "Waking, Dreaming, and Self-Regulation," in *The Functions of Dreaming*, ed. Alan Moffitt, Milton Kramer, and Robert Hoffmann (Albany: State University of New York Press), 197–260.

This led them to the remarkable conclusion: "The present results indicate that the inhibitory constraints on this process are implicit in the organization

NOTES

of the dreamer rather than the dreaming. The lifting of these constraints, their reorganization, can be effected through the mechanisms of attention and intention on what is to be reorganized. The constraints on this response are therefore not implicit in dreaming itself, although this view of dreaming has been widely held." Purcell, Moffitt, and Hoffmann, "Waking, Dreaming, and Self-Regulation," 247.

"Dreams are impartial, spontaneous products": Meredith Sabini, ed., *The Earth Has a Soul: The Nature Writings of C. G. Jung* (Berkeley: North Atlantic Books, 2002), 188.

And yet we already have research findings: See the numerous writings of Jayne Gackenbach.

Chapter 8

"In playing, the child manipulates external phenomena": D. W. Winnicott, *Playing and Reality* (London: Tavistock, 1971), 51.

I have argued elsewhere: Kelly Bulkeley, "Dreaming Is Imaginative Play in Sleep: A Theory of the Function of Dreams," *Dreaming* 29 (2019): 1–23.

But a single, focused case study: This has certainly been true in the history of neuroscience, where the close study of a few individuals (e.g., Phineas Gage, the patient known as H. M.) has enabled huge strides in our understanding of general brain functioning. On this methodological point, I agree with neuroscientist Antonio Damasio in his defense of subjective, introspective reports as valid evidence: "Whether one likes it or not, *all* the contents in our minds are subjective, and the power of science comes from its ability to verify objectively the consistency of many individual subjectivities" (Antonio Damasio, *The Feeling of What Happens: Body and Emotion in the Making of Consciousness* [San Diego, CA: Harcourt, 1999], 83).

"The more I think of it": Robert Louis Stevenson, *Across the Plains* (1900), chapter XIII, https://www.gutenberg.org/ebooks/614.

"Dreamt that my little baby came to life": Paula R. Feldman and Diana Scott-Kilvert, eds., *The Journals of Mary Shelley, 1814–1844*, vol. 1 (New York: Oxford University Press, 1987).

When Gregor Samsa woke up: Franz Kafka, *The Metamorphosis*, trans. Stanley Corngold (New York: W. W. Norton, 1996), 3.

There is a dream which I delight in: Naomi Epel, ed., *Writers Dreaming: 25 Writers Talk about Their Dreams and the Creative Process* (New York: Vintage, 1994), 25.

"A place that's a little like dreaming": Epel, *Writers Dreaming*, 26.

"I don't really get down": Epel, *Writers Dreaming*, 27.

I had a dream that I was back home: Nancy Grace, "Making Dreams into Music: Contemporary Songwriters Carry On an Age-Old Dreaming Tradition," in Bulkeley, *Dreams*, 171.

"A more specific reason": Grace, "Making Dreams into Music," 171.

"Basic conventions of narrative cinema": Philip King, Kelly Bulkeley, and Bernard Welt, *Dreaming in the Classroom: Practices, Methods, and Resources in Dream Education* (Albany: State University of New York Press, 2011), 120.

Its central character experiences: King, Bulkeley, and Welt, *Dreaming in the Classroom*, 128.

Chapter 9

"Retold, my dream is nothing": Jorge Luis Borges, "Nightmares," in *Seven Nights,* trans. Eliot Weinberger (New York: New Directions, 1980), 36.

Findings from cognitive neuroscience: Pierre Maquet, Carlyle Smith, and Robert Stickgold, eds., *Sleep and Brain Plasticity* (New York: Oxford University Press, 2003).

Her method, she said, "was very simple": Calkins, "Statistics of Dreams," 115.

This in itself is meant: After several years of excellent collaboration with the digital design team at Graybox in Portland, Oregon, the SDDb is now managed on the technical side by Sheldon Junker, Daniel Kennedy, and Gez Quinn, the founders of the Elsewhere dream-journaling app. We are working together to integrate their app with the database so the app can build on the resources of the database to boost its value to users, and the database can offer interested, consenting people a portal to participate in dream research projects of many different kinds.

I then compared the results: Including the Hall and Van de Castle Norm dreams plus dream collections gathered by Calvin Hall, Stanley Krippner, Tracey Kahan, and me. For more on the SDDb baselines, see Kelly Bulkeley, *Big Dreams: The Science of Dreaming and the Origins of Religion* (New York: Oxford University Press, 2016).